TENNIS

RESULTS AND STATISTICS

OF THE FOUR GRAND SLAM TOURNAMENTS

Women's Singles and Men's Singles

2015 Edition

Natalie Langlois

Cover pictures by Kevin Langlois ©

Photos taken on October 5th 2015 at Frew Park, Milton, Brisbane, Australia (Officially opened on November 29th 2014)

At that same spot, the old Milton Tennis courts held 8 Australian Championships (which later became the Australian Open), notably in 1915, 1923, 1956, 1960, 1964 and 1969.

Three Davis Cup finals were played at this location in 1958, 1962 and 1967.

Copyright © Nathalie Langlois, December 2015

All rights reserved

To **Spencer Gore,**

and **Maud Watson,**

Wimbledon's FIRST CHAMPIONS
and "pioneers", who were unaware, at the time, of the future worldwide success of tennis.

Thank you to my husband Yves (for his help and patience during the preparation of my book) and to our three sons Jeremy, Kevin and Christopher for their ongoing cheerful contribution!

TABLE OF CONTENTS

TABLE OF CONTENTS 4
INTRODUCTION 6
   QUIZ 7
CHAMPIONS WHO WROTE GRAND SLAM HISTORY 9
AUSTRALIAN OPEN 18
   WOMEN'S SINGLES 18
   ALL WINNERS 21
AUSTRALIAN OPEN 23
   MEN'S SINGLES 23
   ALL WINNERS 27
ROLAND-GARROS 29
   WOMEN'S SINGLES 29
   ALL WINNERS 33
ROLAND-GARROS 35
   MEN'S SINGLES 35
   ALL WINNERS 39
WIMBLEDON 41
   LADIES' SINGLES 41
   ALL WINNERS 45
WIMBLEDON 47
   GENTLEMEN'S SINGLES 47
   ALL WINNERS 52
US OPEN 54
   WOMEN'S SINGLES 54
   ALL WINNERS 58
US OPEN 60
   MEN'S SINGLES 60

    ALL WINNERS 65
TO SUM IT UP 67
RESULT TALLY AND STATISTICS 68
    WOMEN'S RESULTS TALLY (IN ALPHABETICAL ORDER) 68
    MEN'S RESULTS TALLY (IN ALPHABETICAL ORDER) 77
WOMEN'S GRAND SLAM 89
MEN'S GRAND SLAM 92
ALL THE 121 WOMEN CHAMPIONS IN CHRONOLOGICAL ORDER 95
ALL THE 160 MEN CHAMPIONS IN CHRONOLOGICAL ORDER 99
THE 4 GIANTS OF MODERN TENNIS 104
THE SENIORS 105
REPRESENTED COUNTRIES 106
    WOMEN CHAMPIONS 106
    MEN CHAMPIONS 112
    COMBINED WOMEN CHAMPIONS AND MEN CHAMPIONS BY PARTICULAR COUNTRIES 119
    COUNTRIES WITH THE MOST TITLES (WOMEN AND MEN, COMBINED) 121
MORE ON CHAMPIONS 122
    ALL WOMEN CHAMPIONS OVER THE YEARS 122
    ALL MEN CHAMPIONS OVER THE YEARS 131
TWO CHAMPION SURVIVORS OF THE TITANIC 143
    QUIZ: THE ANSWERS 145
CONCLUSION 146

INTRODUCTION

If you are passionate about tennis and the four big championship tournaments in particular, you will find full records for the men's and women's singles finals for every single one of the tournaments in this book.

The intent of this book is not to cover the complete history of the four majors (which has already been covered by many great sports reporters in books providing information and photos)...

Instead, I would like to provide full records related to each tournament from the onset, as well as statistics I have worked out and would like to share with you, for example the number of different champions from the tournaments' history, the seniors, the various champions' nationalities, tallies of the results... as well as some stunning and little known facts.

It was a challenge to name women champions accurately year after year, regardless of whether they were winners or finalists. I have managed to find the champions' maiden and married names according to their wedding date.
I have noticed some documents refer to ladies champions by their married names years before they got married!

A lot of research was required to precisely establish champions' citizenships (for those who have changed citizenship during their careers), in order to accurately identify the country represented for particular victories.

I have also tried my best to provide tie-breaks results which were not necessarily recorded (I am still missing some results).
It is worth noting tie-breaks were initially played at 8 games all, instead of the current 6 games all. This explains set results such as "9-8".

Several finals results are missing from the very beginning of the French Championships, as well as the first names of some early champions (names and results were not recorded accurately then).

The French Championships, which started in 1891, became one of the four major tournaments in 1925, under the name "French International Championships". From 1928 the French Championships were also referred to as the "Roland-Garros tournament". I have listed its champions from 1891 onwards.

Early in the history of the four tournaments, the champions were often locals. Back then, there were not many tennis players and travel constraints were detrimental to players attending overseas tournaments.

I hope you can use this book to quiz your tennis loving friends.

Can you answer the following questions?

QUIZ

- In which final was the first grand slam tie-break played?
- What is the name of the winner of two grand slam singles men titles who also survived the Titanic tragedy?
- How many different champions have won at least one of each grand slam tournament?
- Who was the only champion from New-Zealand to date? (this player died on the battlefields of France during WWI)?
- Who has played at Wimbledon under FOUR different citizenships during his career?
- Who has won his grand slam titles under different citizenships? (Be careful... Don't answer too quickly, this is a difficult question!)
- What is the name of the woman champion who is the mother of another woman champion?
- Who are the woman and man, winners of singles grand slam titles, who became married during their careers? They kept playing singles tournaments for years and also played together in mixed doubles. (Be careful! This is another trick question!).

(By the way... did I tell you the answers are at the end of the book?)

Did you know the US Open ladies' final was played to the best of 5 sets (three sets winner) in 1891, 1892 and from 1894 to 1901?
No less than 5 of these 10 finals were played in 5 sets!
Back then, in the heat of summer, ladies played dressed in long skirts and had to wear heavy underskirts, thick stockings, long sleeve shirts and a large hat.
It is also quite impressive there were no breaks between side changes and no ball kids on the court yet!

How about another commonly unknown statistic?

To this day, in one single calendar year, there have never been 4 new women champions or 4 new men champions, crowned for the first time.

Several times in tennis history, 3 new champions were crowned during a season. The last time was in 2011 for the ladies and in 2003 for the men.

Happy reading and I hope you enjoy remembering the forgotten champions of tennis.

Names of the Four Grand Slam Tennis Tournaments from the beginning:

Australian Open:
. Australasian Championships from 1905 to 1926
. Australian Championships from 1927 to 1968
. Australian Open from 1969 to date.

Roland-Garros:
. French Championships from 1891 to 1924
. International French Championships from 1925 to 1927
. International French Championships OR Roland-Garros from 1928 to date.

Wimbledon: same name since 1877.

US Open:
. US Championships from 1881 to 1967
. US Open from 1968 to date.

CHAMPIONS WHO WROTE GRAND SLAM HISTORY

Ahead of the listing of the tournaments' results, here is the alphabetical list of all champions who have written grand slam history.

If you like this wonderful sport, let's pay them tribute.

I would like to thank them for making millions dream since the first Wimbledon tournament gentlemen's final held on Thursday, July 19, 1877 on a grass field in Surrey.

The 121 Women Champions:

Nelly ADAMSON LANDRY
Daphne AKHURST COZENS
Juliette ATKINSON
Cilly AUSSEM
Tracy AUSTIN
Victoria AZARENKA
Maud BARGER WALLACH
Sue BARKER
Marion BARTOLI
Pauline BETZ ADDIE
Blanche BINGLEY HILLYARD
Molla BJURSTEDT MALLORY
Shirley BLOOMER
Dora BOOTHBY
Kornelia BOUMAN
Esna BOYD ROBERTSON
Marguerite BROQUEDIS
Louise BROUGH CLAPP
Maria BUENO
Dorothy BUNDY CHENEY
Mabel CAHILL
Patricia CANNING TODD
Jennifer CAPRIATI
Mary CARTER REITANO
Kim CLIJSTERS
Maureen CONNOLLY

Charlotte COOPER STERRY
Thelma COYNE LONG
Lindsay DAVENPORT
Lottie DOD
Françoise DURR
Chris EVERT
Shirley FRY IRVIN (Grand Slam's Senior to this day)
Althea GIBSON
Kate GILLOU FENWICK
P. GIROD
Evonne GOOLAGONG-CAWLEY
Steffi GRAF
Ellen HANSELL
Karen HANTZE SUSMAN
Darlene HARD
Doris HART
Joan HARTIGAN BATHURST
Ann HAYDON-JONES
Helen HELLWIG
Justine HENIN
Martina HINGIS
Helen HOMANS
Emily HOOD WESTACOOT
Hazel HOTCHKISS WIGHTMAN
Helen HULL JACOBS
Ana IVANOVIC
Mima JAUSOVEC
Marion JONES FARQUHAR
Barbara JORDAN
Mary KENDALL BROWNE
Thérèse de KERMEL (Countess) (née Villard)
Billie Jean KING (née Moffitt)
Zsuzsa KORMOCZY
Hilde KRAHWINKEL SPERLING
Svetlana KUZNETSOVA
Petra KVITOVA
Dorothea LAMBERT-CHAMBERS (née Douglass)
Sylvia LANCE HARPER

Suzanne LENGLEN
Na LI
Anita LIZANA
Iva MAJOLI
Hana MANDLIKOVA
Alice MARBLE
Conchita MARTINEZ
Adine MASSON
Simonne MATHIEU
Jeanne MATTHEY
Amélie MAURESMO
Myrtle McATEER
Coral McINNES BUTTSWORTH
Kathleen McKANE GODFREE
Kerry MELVILLE REID
Margaret MOLESWORTH
Elisabeth MOORE
Angela MORTIMER
Anastasia MYSKINA
Martina NAVRATILOVA
Jana NOVOTNA
Betty NUTHALL
Chris O'NEIL
Margaret OSBORNE duPONT
Sarah PALFREY COOKE
Flavia PENNETTA
Beryl PENROSE
Mary PIERCE
Hélène PREVOST
Lena RICE
Nancy RICHEY
Muriel ROBB
Ellen ROOSEVELT
Dorothy ROUND LITTLE
Virginia RUZICI
Gabriela SABATINI
Arantxa SANCHEZ VICARIO
Francesca SCHIAVONE

Margaret SCRIVEN
Evelyn SEARS
Monica SELES
Maria SHARAPOVA
Margaret SMITH COURT
Samantha STOSUR
May SUTTON BUNDY
Aline TERRY
Ethel THOMSON LARCOMBE
Bertha TOWNSEND
Christine TRUMAN
Lesley TURNER BOWREY
Julie VLASTO
Virginia WADE
Maud WATSON
Serena WILLIAMS
Venus WILLIAMS
Helen WILLS MOODY
Nancye WYNNE BOLTON

There are **121** women champions who have won at least one grand slam tournament.

Of these 121 champions, only 9 are still playing to this day:

Victoria Azarenka, Ana Ivanovic, Svetlana Kuznetsova, Petra Kvitova, Francesca Schiavone, Maria Sharapova, Samantha Stosur, Serena Williams and Venus Williams.

To date, **448** women's tennis grand slam tournaments have been played (including the 2015 US Open).

The 160 Men Champions:

Andre AGASSI
Fred ALEXANDER
Wilmer ALLISON
James ANDERSON
Mal ANDERSON
Jozsef ASBOTH
Arthur ASHE
Paul AYME
Wilfred BADDELEY
Boris BECKER
Marcel BERNARD
François BLANCHY
Björn BORG
Jean BOROTRA
Bill BOWREY
H. BRIGGS
John BROMWICH
Norman BROOKES
Sergi BRUGUERA
Donald BUDGE
Oliver CAMPBELL
Pat CASH
Michael CHANG
Marin CILIC
William CLOTHIER
Henri COCHET
Jimmy CONNORS
Ashley COOPER
Albert COSTA
Jim COURIER
Jack CRAWFORD
Sven DAVIDSON
Max DECUGIS
Juan Martin DEL POTRO
Novak DJOKOVIC
John DOEG

Laurie DOHERTY
Reggie DOHERTY
Jaroslav DROBNY
Stefan EDBERG
Mark EDMONDSON
Roy EMERSON
Bob FALKENBURG
Roger FEDERER
Juan Carlos FERRERO
Neale FRASER
Gaston GAUDIO
Rhys GEMMELL
Maurice GERMOT
Vitas GERULAITIS
Andres GIMENO
André GOBERT
Andres GOMEZ
Pancho GONZALEZ
Arthur GORE
Spencer GORE
Colin GREGORY
Frank HADOW
Willoughby HAMILTON
John HARTLEY
John HAWKES
Rodney HEATH
Henner HENKEL
Lleyton HEWITT
Lewis HOAD
Fred HOVEY
Joseph HUNT
Goran IVANISEVIC
Thomas JOHANSSON
Bill JOHNSTON
Yevgeny KAFELNIKOV
Algernon KINGSCOTE
Jan KODES
Petr KORDA

Richard KRAJICEK
Jack KRAMER
Johan KRIEK
Gustavo KUERTEN
René LACOSTE
William LARNED
Arthur LARSEN
Rod LAVER
Herbert LAWFORD
Ivan LENDL
Gordon LOWE
Harold MAHONY
John McENROE
Vivian McGRATH
Ken McGREGOR
Chuck McKINLEY
Maurice McLOUGHLIN
William McNEILL
Edgar MOON
Carlos MOYA
Andy MURRAY
Robert Lindley MURRAY
Thomas MUSTER
Rafael NADAL
Ilie NASTASE
John NEWCOMBE
Yannick NOAH
Arthur O'HARA WOOD
Pat O'HARA WOOD
Alex OLMEDO
Manuel ORANTES
Rafael OSUNA
Dinny PAILS
Adriano PANATTA
James PARKE
Ernie PARKER
Frank PARKER
Gerald PATTERSON

Budge PATTY
Fred PERRY
Yvon PETRA
Nicola PIETRANGELI
Joshua PIM
Adrian QUIST
Patrick RAFTER
Ernest RENSHAW
William RENSHAW
Laurent RIBOULET
Horace RICE
Bobby RIGGS
Tony ROCHE
Andy RODDICK
Mervyn ROSE
Ken ROSEWALL
Marat SAFIN
Jean SAMAZEUILH
Pete SAMPRAS
Manuel SANTANA
Dick SAVITT
Jean SCHOPFER
Ted SCHROEDER
Richard SEARS
Frank SEDGMAN
Vic SEIXAS (Grand Slam's Senior to this day)
Henry SLOCUM
Stan SMITH
Michael STICH
Fred STOLLE
Roscoe TANNER
Brian TEACHER
William TILDEN
Tony TRABERT
André VACHEROT
Michel VACHEROT
Guillermo VILAS
Ellsworth VINES

Gottfried von CRAMM (Baron)
Holcombe WARD
Stanislas WAWRINKA
Malcolm WHITMAN
Mats WILANDER
Tony WILDING
Richard Norris WILLIAMS
Sidney WOOD
Robert WRENN
Beals WRIGHT

There are **160** men champions who have won at least one grand slam tournament.

Of these 160 champions, only 8 are still playing to this day:

Marin Cilic, Juan Martin Del Potro, Novak Djokovic, Roger Federer, Lleyton Hewitt, Andy Murray, Rafael Nadal and Stanislas Wawrinka.

To date, **481** men's tennis grand slam tournaments have been played (including 2015 US Open).

AUSTRALIAN OPEN

Women's Singles

Australasian Championships

1922: Margaret Molesworth def. Esna Boyd Robertson 6-3, 10-8
1923: Margaret Molesworth def. Esna Boyd Robertson 6-1, 7-5
1924: Sylvia Lance Harper def. Esna Boyd Robertson 6-3, 3-6, 6-4
1925: Daphne Akhurst Cozens def. Esna Boyd Robertson 1-6, 8-6, 6-4
1926: Daphne Akhurst Cozens def. Esna Boyd Robertson 6-1, 6-3

Australian Championships

1927: Esna Boyd Robertson def. Sylvia Lance Harper 5-7, 6-1, 6-2
1928: Daphne Akhurst Cozens def. Esna Boyd Robertson 7-5, 6-2
1929: Daphne Akhurst Cozens def. Louie Bickerton 6-1, 5-7, 6-2
1930: Daphne Akhurst Cozens def. Sylvia Lance Harper 10-8, 2-6, 7-5
1931: Coral McInnes Buttsworth def. Marjorie Cox Crawford 1-6, 6-3, 6-4
1932: Coral McInnes Buttsworth def. Kathrine Le Messurier 9-7, 6-4
1933: Joan Hartigan Bathurst def. Coral McInnes Buttsworth 6-4, 6-3
1934: Joan Hartigan Bathurst def. Margaret Molesworth 6-1, 6-4
1935: Dorothy Round Little def. Nancy Lyle 1-6, 6-1, 6-3
1936: Joan Hartigan Bathurst def. Nancye Wynne Bolton 6-4, 6-4
1937: Nancye Wynne Bolton def. Emily Hood Westacott 6-3, 5-7, 6-4
1938: Dorothy Bundy def. Dorothy Stevenson 6-3, 6-2
1939: Emily Hood Westacoot def. Nell Hall Hopman 6-1, 6-2
1940: Nancye Wynne Bolton def. Thelma Coyne Long 5-7, 6-4, 6-0
1941 to 1945: no competition (due to WWII)
1946: Nancye Wynne Bolton def. Joyce Fitch 6-4, 6-4
1947: Nancye Wynne Bolton def. Nell Hall Hopman 6-3, 6-2
1948: Nancye Wynne Bolton def. Marie Toomey 6-3, 6-1
1949: Doris Hart def. Nancye Wynne Bolton 6-3, 6-4
1950: Louise Brough Clapp def. Doris Hart 6-4, 3-6, 6-4
1951: Nancye Wynne Bolton def. Thelma Coyne Long 6-1, 7-5
1952: Thelma Coyne Long def. Helen Angwin 6-2, 6-3
1953: Maureen Connolly def. Julia Ann Sampson 6-3, 6-2

1954: Thelma Coyne Long def. Jenny Staley 6-3, 6-4
1955: Beryl Penrose def. Thelma Coyne Long 6-4, 6-3
1956: Mary Carter Reitano def. Thelma Coyne Long 3-6, 6-2, 9-7
1957: Shirley Fry Irvin def. Althea Gibson 6-3, 6-4
1958: Angela Mortimer def. Lorraine Coghlan 6-3, 6-4
1959: Mary Carter Reitano def. Renee Schuurman 6-2, 6-3
1960: Margaret Smith def. Jan Lehane 7-5, 6-2
1961: Margaret Smith def. Jan Lehane O'Neill 6-1, 6-4
1962: Margaret Smith def. Jan Lehane O'Neill 6-0, 6-2
1963: Margaret Smith def. Jan Lehane O'Neill 6-2, 6-2
1964: Margaret Smith def. Lesley Turner 6-3, 6-2
1965: Margaret Smith def. Maria Bueno 5-7, 6-4, 5-2 ret.
1966: Margaret Smith def. Nancy Richey, walkover
1967: Nancy Richey def. Lesley Turner 6-1, 6-4
1968: Billie Jean King def. Margaret Smith Court 6-1, 6-2

Open Era

1969: Margaret Smith Court def. Billie Jean King 6-4, 6-1
1970: Margaret Smith Court def. Kerry Melville 6-3, 6-1
1971: Margaret Smith Court def. Evonne Goolagong 2-6, 7-6^0, 7-5
1972: Virginia Wade def. Evonne Goolagong 6-4, 6-4
1973: Margaret Smith Court def. Evonne Goolagong 6-4, 7-5
1974: Evonne Goolagong def. Chris Evert 7-6^5, 4-6, 6-0
1975: Evonne Goolagong-Cawley def. Martina Navratilova 6-3, 6-2
1976: Evonne Goolagong-Cawley def. Renata Tomanova 6-2, 6-2
1977 (January): Kerry Melville Reid def. Dianne Fromholtz Balestrat 7-5, 6-2
1977 (December): Evonne Goolagong-Cawley def. Helen Gourlay-Cawley 6-3, 6-0
1978: Chris O'Neil def. Betsy Nagelsen 6-3, 7-6^3
1979: Barbara Jordan def. Sharon Walsh 6-3, 6-3
1980: Hana Mandlikova def. Wendy Turnbull 6-0, 7-5
1981: Martina Navratilova def. Chris Evert-Lloyd 6-7^4, 6-4, 7-5
1982: Chris Evert-Lloyd def. Martina Navratilova 6-3, 2-6, 6-3
1983: Martina Navratilova def. Kathy Jordan 6-2, 7-6^5
1984: Chris Evert-Lloyd def. Helena Sukova 6-7^4, 6-1, 6-3
1985: Martina Navratilova def. Chris Evert-Lloyd 6-2, 4-6, 6-2
1986: no competition*
1987: Hana Mandlikova def. Martina Navratilova 7-5, 7-6^1

1988: Steffi Graf def. Chris Evert 6-1, 7-6^3
1989: Steffi Graf def. Helena Sukova 6-4, 6-4
1990: Steffi Graf def. Mary Joe Fernandez 6-3, 6-4
1991: Monica Seles def. Jana Novotna 5-7, 6-3, 6-1
1992: Monica Seles def. Mary Joe Fernandez 6-2, 6-3
1993: Monica Seles def. Steffi Graf 4-6, 6-3, 6-2
1994: Steffi Graf def. Arantxa Sanchez Vicario 6-0, 6-2
1995: Mary Pierce def. Arantxa Sanchez Vicario 6-3, 6-2
1996: Monica Seles def. Anke Huber 6-4, 6-1
1997: Martina Hingis def. Mary Pierce 6-2, 6-2
1998: Martina Hingis def. Conchita Martinez 6-3, 6-3
1999: Martina Hingis def. Amélie Mauresmo 6-2, 6-3
2000: Lindsay Davenport def. Martina Hingis 6-1, 7-5
2001: Jennifer Capriati def. Martina Hingis 6-4, 6-3
2002: Jennifer Capriati def. Martina Hingis 4-6, 7-6^7, 6-2
2003: Serena Williams def. Venus Williams 7-6^4, 3-6, 6-4
2004: Justine Henin-Hardenne def. Kim Clijsters 6-3, 4-6, 6-3
2005: Serena Williams def. Lindsay Davenport Leach 2-6, 6-3, 6-0
2006: Amélie Mauresmo def. Justine Henin-Hardenne 6-1, 2-0 ret.
2007: Serena Williams def. Maria Sharapova 6-1, 6-2
2008: Maria Sharapova def. Ana Ivanovic 7-5, 6-3
2009: Serena Williams def. Dinara Safina 6-0, 6-3
2010: Serena Williams def. Justine Henin 6-4, 3-6, 6-2
2011: Kim Clijsters Lynch def. Li Na 3-6, 6-3, 6-3
2012: Victoria Azarenka def. Maria Sharapova 6-3, 6-0
2013: Victoria Azarenka def. Li Na 4-6, 6-4, 6-3
2014: Li Na def. Dominika Cibulkova 7-6^3, 6-0
2015: Serena Williams def. Maria Sharapova 6-3, 7-6^5

*In 1977, a decision was made to re-schedule the Australian Open from January to December. Therefore, two Australian Open tournaments were played in 1977. The tournament was held in December up until 1985, when the tournament was brought back to the month of January. This lead to the tournament not being played at all during 1986. The Australian Open has been played in January since 1987.

All winners

1: Margaret Molesworth (1922, 1923)
2: Sylvia Lance Harper (1924)
3: Daphne Akhurst Cozens (1925, 1926, 1928, 1929, 1930)
4: Esna Boyd Robertson (1927)
5: Coral McInnes Buttsworth (1931, 1932)
6: Joan Hartigan Bathurst (1933, 1934, 1936)
7: Dorothy Round Little (1935)
8: Nancye Wynne Bolton (1937, 1940, 1946, 1947, 1948, 1951)
9: Dorothy Bundy (1938)
10: Emily Hood Westacoot (1939)
11: Doris Hart (1949)
12: Louise Brough Clapp (1950)
13: Thelma Coyne Long (1952, 1954)
14: Maureen Connolly (1953)
15: Beryl Penrose (1955)
16: Mary Carter Reitano (1956, 1959)
17: Shirley Fry Irvin (1957) (tournament's Senior to this day)
18: Angela Mortimer (1958)
19: Margaret Smith (then wed. Court) (1960, 1961, 1962, 1963, 1964, 1965, 1966, 1969, 1970, 1971, 1973)
20: Nancy Richey (1967)
21: Billie Jean King (1968)
22: Virginia Wade (1972)
23: Evonne Goolagong (then wed. Cawley) (1974, 1975, 1976, 1977 December)
24: Kerry Melville Reid (1977 January)
25: Chris O'Neil (1978)
26: Barbara Jordan (1979)
27: Hana Mandlikova (1980, 1987)
28: Martina Navratilova (1981, 1983, 1985)
29: Chris Evert-Lloyd (1982, 1984)
30: Steffi Graf (1988, 1989, 1990, 1994)
31: Monica Seles (1991, 1992, 1993, 1996)
32: Mary Pierce (1995)
33: Martina Hingis (1997, 1998, 1999)
34: Lindsay Davenport (2000)
35: Jennifer Capriati (2001, 2002)

36: Serena Williams (2003, 2005, 2007, 2009, 2010, 2015)
37: Justine Henin (2004)
38: Amélie Mauresmo (2006)
39: Maria Sharapova (2008)
40: Kim Clijsters Lynch (2011)
41: Victoria Azarenka (2012, 2013)
42: Li Na (2014)

89 tournaments have been played.

Champions who were single at the time of their first victory have been listed under their maiden names. Their married names are quoted in brackets.

The tournament's senior is Shirley Fry Irvin, from the USA, 17th champion in 1957, born June 30, 1927 (88 years old).

AUSTRALIAN OPEN

Men's Singles

Australasian Championships

1905: Rodney Heath def. Arthur Curtis 4-6, 6-3, 6-4, 6-4
1906: Tony Wilding def. Francis Fisher 6-0, 6-4, 6-4
1907: Horace Rice def. Harry Parker 6-3, 6-4, 6-4
1908: Fred Alexander def. Alfred Dunlop 3-6, 3-6, 6-0, 6-2, 6-3
1909: Tony Wilding def. Ernie Parker 6-1, 7-5, 6-2
1910: Rodney Heath def. Horace Rice 6-4, 6-3, 6-2
1911: Norman Brookes def. Horace Rice 6-1, 6-2, 6-3
1912: James Parke def. Alfred Beamish 3-6, 6-3, 1-6, 6-1, 7-5
1913: Ernie Parker def. Harry Parker 2-6, 6-1, 6-2, 6-3
1914: Arthur O'Hara Wood def. Gerald Patterson 6-4, 6-3, 5-7, 6-1
1915: Gordon Lowe def. Horace Rice 4-6, 6-1, 6-1, 6-4
1916 to 1918: no competition (due to WWI)
1919: Algernon Kingscote def. Eric Pockley 6-4, 6-0, 6-3
1920: Pat O'Hara Wood def. Ronald Thomas 6-3, 4-6, 6-8, 6-1, 6-3
1921: Rhys Gemmell def. Alfred Hedeman 7-5, 6-1, 6-4
1922: James Anderson def. Gerald Patterson 6-0, 3-6, 3-6, 6-3, 6-2
1923: Pat O'Hara Wood def. Bert St. John 6-1, 6-1, 6-3
1924: James Anderson def. Richard Schlesinger 6-3, 6-4, 3-6, 5-7, 6-3
1925: James Anderson def. Gerald Patterson 11-9, 2-6, 6-2, 6-3
1926: John Hawkes def. Jim Willard 6-1, 6-3, 6-1

Australian Championships

1927: Gerald Patterson def. John Hawkes 3-6, 6-4, 3-6, 18-16, 6-3
1928: Jean Borotra def. Jack Cummings 6-4, 6-1, 4-6, 5-7, 6-3
1929: Colin Gregory def. Richard Schlesinger 6-2, 6-2, 5-7, 7-5
1930: Edgar Moon def. Harry Hopman 6-3, 6-1, 6-3
1931: Jack Crawford def. Harry Hopman 6-4, 6-2, 2-6, 6-1
1932: Jack Crawford def. Harry Hopman 4-6, 6-3, 3-6, 6-3, 6-1
1933: Jack Crawford def. Keith Gledhill 2-6, 7-5, 6-3, 6-2
1934: Fred Perry def. Jack Crawford 6-3, 7-5, 6-1

1935: Jack Crawford def. Fred Perry 2-6, 6-4, 6-4, 6-4
1936: Adrian Quist def. Jack Crawford 6-2, 6-3, 4-6, 3-6, 9-7
1937: Vivian McGrath def. John Bromwich 6-3, 1-6, 6-0, 2-6, 6-1
1938: Donald Budge def. John Bromwich 6-4, 6-2, 6-1
1939: John Bromwich def. Adrian Quist 6-4, 6-1, 6-3
1940: Adrian Quist def. Jack Crawford 6-3, 6-1, 6-2
1941 to 1945: no competition (due to WWII)
1946: John Bromwich def. Dinny Pails 5-7, 6-3, 7-5, 3-6, 6-2
1947: Dinny Pails def. John Bromwich 4-6, 6-4, 3-6, 7-5, 8-6
1948: Adrian Quist def. John Bromwich 6-4, 3-6, 6-3, 2-6, 6-3
1949: Frank Sedgman def. John Bromwich 6-3, 6-3, 6-2
1950: Frank Sedgman def. Ken McGregor 6-3, 6-4, 4-6, 6-1
1951: Dick Savitt def. Ken McGregor 6-3, 2-6, 6-3, 6-1
1952: Ken McGregor def. Frank Sedgman 7-5, 12-10, 2-6, 6-2
1953: Ken Rosewall def. Mervyn Rose 6-0, 6-3, 6-4
1954: Mervyn Rose def. Rex Hartwig 6-2, 0-6, 6-4, 6-2
1955: Ken Rosewall def. Lewis Hoad 9-7, 6-4, 6-4
1956: Lewis Hoad def. Ken Rosewall 6-4, 3-6, 6-4, 7-5
1957: Ashley Cooper def. Neale Fraser 6-3, 9-11, 6-4, 6-2
1958: Ashley Cooper def. Mal Anderson 7-5, 6-3, 6-4
1959: Alex Olmedo def. Neale Fraser 6-1, 6-2, 3-6, 6-3
1960: Rod Laver def. Neale Fraser 5-7, 3-6, 6-3, 8-6, 8-6
1961: Roy Emerson def. Rod Laver 1-6, 6-3, 7-5, 6-4
1962: Rod Laver def. Roy Emerson 8-6, 0-6, 6-4, 6-4
1963: Roy Emerson def. Ken Fletcher 6-3, 6-3, 6-1
1964: Roy Emerson def. Fred Stolle 6-3, 6-4, 6-2
1965: Roy Emerson def. Fred Stolle 7-9, 2-6, 6-4, 7-5, 6-1
1966: Roy Emerson def. Arthur Ashe 6-4, 6-8, 6-2, 6-3
1967: Roy Emerson def. Arthur Ashe 6-4, 6-1, 6-1
1968: Bill Bowrey def. Juan Gisbert 7-5, 2-6, 9-7, 6-4

Open Era

1969: Rod Laver def. Andres Gimeno 6-3, 6-4, 7-5
1970: Arthur Ashe def. Dick Crealy 6-4, 9-7, 6-2
1971: Ken Rosewall def. Arthur Ashe 6-1, 7-5, 6-3
1972: Ken Rosewall def. Mal Anderson 7-6^2, 6-3, 7-5
1973: John Newcombe def. Onny Parun 6-3, 6-7, 7-5, 6-1

1974: Jimmy Connors def. Phil Dent 7-6^7, 6-4, 4-6, 6-3
1975: John Newcombe def. Jimmy Connors 7-5, 3-6, 6-4, 7-6^7
1976: Mark Edmondson def. John Newcombe 6-7, 6-3, 7-6, 6-1
1977 (January): Roscoe Tanner def. Guillermo Vilas 6-3, 6-3, 6-3
1977 (December): Vitas Gerulaitis def. John Lloyd 6-3, 7-6^1, 5-7, 3-6, 6-2
1978: Guillermo Vilas def. John Marks 6-4, 6-4, 3-6, 6-3
1979: Guillermo Vilas def. John Sadri 7-6^4, 6-3, 6-2
1980: Brian Teacher def. Kim Warwick 7-5, 7-6^4, 6-3
1981: Johan Kriek def. Steve Denton 6-2, 7-6^1, 6-7^1, 6-4
1982: Johan Kriek def. Steve Denton 6-3, 6-3, 6-2
1983: Mats Wilander def. Ivan Lendl 6-1, 6-4, 6-4
1984: Mats Wilander def. Kevin Curren 6-7^5, 6-4, 7-6^3, 6-2
1985: Stefan Edberg def. Mats Wilander 6-4, 6-3, 6-3
1986: no competition*
1987: Stefan Edberg def. Pat Cash 6-3, 6-4, 3-6, 5-7, 6-3
1988: Mats Wilander def. Pat Cash 6-3, 6-7^3, 3-6, 6-1, 8-6
1989: Ivan Lendl def. Miloslav Mecir 6-2, 6-2, 6-2
1990: Ivan Lendl def. Stefan Edberg 4-6, 7-6^3, 5-2, ret.
1991: Boris Becker def. Ivan Lendl 1-6, 6-4, 6-4, 6-4
1992: Jim Courier def. Stefan Edberg 6-3, 3-6, 6-4, 6-2
1993: Jim Courier def. Stefan Edberg 6-2, 6-1, 2-6, 7-5
1994: Pete Sampras def. Todd Martin 7-6^4, 6-4, 6-4
1995: Andre Agassi def. Pete Sampras 4-6, 6-1, 7-6^6, 6-4
1996: Boris Becker def. Michael Chang 6-2, 6-4, 2-6, 6-4
1997: Pete Sampras def. Carlos Moya 6-2, 6-3, 6-3
1998: Petr Korda def. Marcelo Rios 6-2, 6-2, 6-2
1999: Yevgeny Kafelnikov def. Thomas Enqvist 4-6, 6-0, 6-3, 7-6^1
2000: Andre Agassi def. Yevgeny Kafelnikov 3-6, 6-3, 6-2, 6-4
2001: Andre Agassi def. Arnaud Clément 6-4, 6-2, 6-2
2002: Thomas Johansson def. Marat Safin 3-6, 6-4, 6-4, 7-6^4
2003: Andre Agassi def. Rainer Schüttler 6-2, 6-2, 6-1
2004: Roger Federer def. Marat Safin 7-6^3, 6-4, 6-3
2005: Marat Safin def. Lleyton Hewitt 1-6, 6-3, 6-4, 6-4
2006: Roger Federer def. Marcos Baghdatis 5-7, 7-5, 6-0, 6-2
2007: Roger Federer def. Fernando Gonzalez 7-6^2, 6-4, 6-4
2008: Novak Djokovic def. Jo-Wilfried Tsonga 4-6, 6-4, 6-3, 7-6^2
2009: Rafael Nadal def. Roger Federer 7-5, 3-6, 7-6^3, 3-6, 6-2
2010: Roger Federer def. Andy Murray 6-3, 6-4, 7-6^{11}

2011: Novak Djokovic def. Andy Murray 6-4, 6-2, 6-3
2012: Novak Djokovic def. Rafael Nadal 5-7, 6-4, 6-2, 6-7^5, 7-5
2013: Novak Djokovic def. Andy Murray 6-7^2, 7-6^3, 6-3, 6-2
2014: Stanislas Wawrinka def. Rafael Nadal 6-3, 6-2, 3-6, 6-3
2015: Novak Djokovic def. Andy Murray 7-6^5, 6-7^4, 6-3, 6-0

*In 1977, a decision was made to re-schedule the Australian Open from January to December. Therefore, two Australian Open tournaments were played in 1977. The tournament was held in December up until 1985, when the tournament was brought back to the month of January. This lead to the tournament not being played at all during 1986. The Australian Open has been played in January since 1987.

All winners

1: Rodney Heath (1905, 1910)
2: Tony Wilding (1906, 1909)
3: Horace Rice (1907)
4: Fred Alexander (1908)
5: Norman Brookes (1911)
6: James Parke (1912)
7: Ernie Parker (1913)
8: Arthur O'Hara Wood (1914)
9: Gordon Lowe (1915)
10: Algernon Kingscote (1919)
11: Pat O'Hara Wood (1920, 1923)
12: Rhys Gemmell (1921)
13: James Anderson (1922, 1924, 1925)
14: John Hawkes (1926)
15: Gerald Patterson (1927)
16: Jean Borotra (1928)
17: Colin Gregory (1929)
18: Edgar Moon (1930)
19: Jack Crawford (1931, 1932, 1933, 1935)
20: Fred Perry (1934)
21: Adrian Quist (1936, 1940, 1948)
22: Vivian McGrath (1937)
23: Donald Budge (1938)
24: John Bromwich (1939, 1946)
25: Dinny Pails (1947)
26: Frank Sedgman (1949, 1950)
27: Dick Savitt (1951) (tournament's Senior to this day)
28: Ken McGregor (1952)
29: Ken Rosewall (1953, 1955, 1971, 1972)
30: Mervyn Rose (1954)
31: Lewis Hoad (1956)
32: Ashley Cooper (1957, 1958)
33: Alex Olmedo (1959)
34: Rod Laver (1960, 1962, 1969)
35: Roy Emerson (1961, 1963, 1964, 1965, 1966, 1967)
36: Bill Bowrey (1968)

37: Arthur Ashe (1970)
38: John Newcombe (1973, 1975)
39: Jimmy Connors (1974)
40: Mark Edmondson (1976)
41: Roscoe Tanner (1977 January)
42: Vitas Gerulaitis (1977 December)
43: Guillermo Vilas (1978, 1979)
44: Brian Teacher (1980)
45: Johan Kriek (1981, 1982)
46: Mats Wilander (1983, 1984, 1988)
47: Stefan Edberg (1985, 1987)
48: Ivan Lendl (1989, 1990)
49: Boris Becker (1991, 1996)
50: Jim Courier (1992, 1993)
51: Pete Sampras (1994, 1997)
52: Andre Agassi (1995, 2000, 2001, 2003)
53: Petr Korda (1998)
54: Yevgeny Kafelnikov (1999)
55: Thomas Johansson (2002)
56: Roger Federer (2004, 2006, 2007, 2010)
57: Marat Safin (2005)
58: Novak Djokovic (2008, 2011, 2012, 2013, 2015)
59: Rafael Nadal (2009)
60: Stanislas Wawrinka (2014)

103 tournaments have been played.

The tournament's senior is Dick Savitt, from the USA, 27th champion in 1951, born March 4, 1927 (88 years old).

ROLAND-GARROS

Women's Singles

French Championships

1897: Adine Masson def. P. Girod 6-3, 6-1
1898: Adine Masson (no final)
1899: Adine Masson (no final)
1900: Hélène Prévost (no final)
1901: P. Girod def. Leroux 6-1, 6-1
1902: Adine Masson def. P. Girod 6-4, 6-2
1903: Adine Masson def. Kate Gillou 6-0, 6-8, 6-0
1904: Kate Gillou def. Adine Masson
1905: Kate Gillou def. Yvonne de Pfeffel 6-0, 11-9
1906: Kate Gillou-Fenwick def. Virginia Mac Veagh
1907: Countess Thérèse de Kermel def. Catherine d'Aliney d'Elva 6-1, ret.
1908: Kate Gillou-Fenwick def. A. Péan 6-2, 6-2
1909: Jeanne Matthey def. Abeille Villard Gallay 10-8, 6-4
1910: Jeanne Matthey def. Germaine Régnier Golding 1-6, 6-1, 9-7
1911: Jeanne Matthey def. Marguerite Broquedis 6-2, 7-5
1912: Jeanne Matthey def. Marie Danet 6-2, 7-5
1913: Marguerite Broquedis def. Jeanne Matthey 6-3, 6-3
1914: Marguerite Broquedis def. Suzanne Lenglen 5-7, 6-4, 6-3
1915 to 1919: no competition (due to WWI)
1920: Suzanne Lenglen def. Marguerite Broquedis 6-1, 7-5
1921: Suzanne Lenglen def. Germaine Régnier Golding, walkover
1922: Suzanne Lenglen def. Germaine Régnier Golding 6-4, 6-0
1923: Suzanne Lenglen def. Germaine Régnier Golding 6-1, 6-4
1924: Julie Vlasto def. Jeanne Vaussard 6-2, 6-3

International French Championships

1925: Suzanne Lenglen def. Kathleen McKane Godfree 6-1, 6-2
1926: Suzanne Lenglen def. Mary Kendall Browne 6-1, 6-0
1927: Kornelia Bouman def. Irene Bowder Peacock 6-2, 6-4
1928: Helen Wills def. Eileen Bennett 6-1, 6-2 **(First year at Roland-Garros Stadium)**

1929: Helen Wills def. Simonne Mathieu 6-3, 6-4
1930: Helen Wills Moody def. Helen Hull Jacobs 6-2, 6-1
1931: Cilly Aussem def. Betty Nuthall 8-6, 6-1
1932: Helen Wills Moody def. Simonne Mathieu 7-5, 6-1
1933: Margaret Scriven def. Simonne Mathieu 6-2, 4-6, 6-4
1934: Margaret Scriven def. Helen Hull Jacobs 7-5, 4-6, 6-1
1935: Hilde Krahwinkel Sperling def. Simonne Mathieu 6-2, 6-1
1936: Hilde Krahwinkel Sperling def. Simonne Mathieu 6-3, 6-4
1937: Hilde Krahwinkel Sperling def. Simonne Mathieu 6-2, 6-4
1938: Simonne Mathieu def. Nelly Adamson Landry 6-0, 6-3
1939: Simonne Mathieu def. Jadwiga Jedrzejowska 6-3, 8-6
1940 to 1945: no competition (due to WWII)
1946: Margaret Osborne def. Pauline Betz Addie 1-6, 8-6, 7-5
1947: Patricia Canning Todd def. Doris Hart 6-3, 3-6, 6-4
1948: Nelly Adamson Landry def. Shirley Fry Irvin 6-2, 0-6, 6-0
1949: Margaret Osborne duPont def. Nelly Adamson Landry 7-5, 6-2
1950: Doris Hart def. Patricia Canning Todd 6-4, 4-6, 6-2
1951: Shirley Fry Irvin def. Doris Hart 6-3, 3-6, 6-3
1952: Doris Hart def. Shirley Fry Irvin 6-4, 6-4
1953: Maureen Connolly def. Doris Hart 6-2, 6-4
1954: Maureen Connolly def. Ginette Jucker Bucaille 6-4, 6-1
1955: Angela Mortimer def. Dorothy Head Knode 2-6, 7-5, 10-8
1956: Althea Gibson def. Angela Mortimer 6-0, 12-10
1957: Shirley Bloomer def. Dorothy Head Knode 6-1, 6-3
1958: Zsuzsa Kormoczy def. Shirley Bloomer 6-4, 1-6, 6-2
1959: Christine Truman def. Zsuzsa Kormoczy 6-4, 7-5
1960: Darlene Hard def. Yola Ramirez Ochoa 6-3, 6-4
1961: Ann Haydon-Jones def. Yola Ramirez Ochoa 6-2, 6-1
1962: Margaret Smith def. Lesley Turner 6-3, 3-6, 7-5
1963: Lesley Turner def. Ann Haydon-Jones 2-6, 6-3, 7-5
1964: Margaret Smith def. Maria Bueno 5-7, 6-1, 6-2
1965: Lesley Turner def. Margaret Smith 6-3, 6-4
1966: Ann Haydon-Jones def. Nancy Richey 6-3, 6-1
1967: Françoise Durr def. Lesley Turner 4-6, 6-3, 6-4

Open Era

1968: Nancy Richey def. Ann Haydon-Jones 5-7, 6-4, 6-1

1969: Margaret Smith Court def. Ann Haydon-Jones 6-1, 4-6, 6-3
1970: Margaret Smith Court def. Helga Niessen Masthoff 6-2, 6-4
1971: Evonne Goolagong def. Helen Gourlay-Cawley 6-3, 7-5
1972: Billie Jean King def. Evonne Goolagong 6-3, 6-3
1973: Margaret Smith Court def. Chris Evert 6-7, 7-6, 6-4
1974: Chris Evert def. Olga Morozova 6-1, 6-2
1975: Chris Evert def. Martina Navratilova 2-6, 6-2, 6-1
1976: Sue Barker def. Renata Tomanova 6-2, 0-6, 6-2
1977: Mima Jausovec def. Florenta Mihai 6-2, 6-7, 6-1
1978: Virginia Ruzici def. Mima Jausovec 6-2, 6-2
1979: Chris Evert-Lloyd def. Wendy Turnbull 6-2, 6-0
1980: Chris Evert-Lloyd def. Virginia Ruzici 6-0, 6-3
1981: Hana Mandlikova def. Sylvia Hanika 6-2, 6-4
1982: Martina Navratilova def. Andrea Jaeger 7-6^6, 6-1
1983: Chris Evert-Lloyd def. Mima Jausovec 6-1, 6-2
1984: Martina Navratilova def. Chris Evert-Lloyd 6-3, 6-1
1985: Chris Evert-Lloyd def. Martina Navratilova 6-3, 6-7^4, 7-5
1986: Chris Evert-Lloyd def. Martina Navratilova 2-6, 6-3, 6-3
1987: Steffi Graf def. Martina Navratilova 6-4, 4-6, 8-6
1988: Steffi Graf def. Natasha Zvereva 6-0, 6-0
1989: Arantxa Sanchez Vicario def. Steffi Graf 7-6^6, 3-6, 7-5
1990: Monica Seles def. Steffi Graf 7-6^6, 6-4
1991: Monica Seles def. Arantxa Sanchez Vicario 6-3, 6-4
1992: Monica Seles def. Steffi Graf 6-2, 3-6, 10-8
1993: Steffi Graf def. Mary Joe Fernandez 4-6, 6-2, 6-4
1994: Arantxa Sanchez Vicario def. Mary Pierce 6-4, 6-4
1995: Steffi Graf def. Arantxa Sanchez Vicario 7-5, 4-6, 6-0
1996: Steffi Graf def. Arantxa Sanchez Vicario 6-3, 6-7^4, 10-8
1997: Iva Majoli def. Martina Hingis 6-4, 6-2
1998: Arantxa Sanchez Vicario def. Monica Seles 7-6^5, 0-6, 6-2
1999: Steffi Graf def. Martina Hingis 4-6, 7-5, 6-2
2000: Mary Pierce def. Conchita Martinez 6-2, 7-5
2001: Jennifer Capriati def. Kim Clijsters 1-6, 6-4, 12-10
2002: Serena Williams def. Venus Williams 7-5, 6-3
2003: Justine Henin-Hardenne def. Kim Clijsters 6-0, 6-4
2004: Anastasia Myskina def. Elena Dementieva 6-1, 6-2
2005: Justine Henin-Hardenne def. Mary Pierce 6-1, 6-1
2006: Justine Henin-Hardenne def. Svetlana Kuznetsova 6-4, 6-4

2007: Justine Henin def. Ana Ivanovic 6-1, 6-2
2008: Ana Ivanovic def. Dinara Safina 6-4, 6-3
2009: Svetlana Kuznetsova def. Dinara Safina 6-4, 6-2
2010: Francesca Schiavone def. Samantha Stosur 6-4, 7-6^2
2011: Li Na def. Francesca Schiavone 6-4, 7-6^0
2012: Maria Sharapova def. Sara Errani 6-3, 6-2
2013: Serena Williams def. Maria Sharapova 6-4, 6-4
2014: Maria Sharapova def. Simona Halep 6-4, 6-7^5, 6-4
2015: Serena Williams def. Lucie Safarova 6-3, 6-7^2, 6-2

All winners

1: Adine Masson (1897, 1898, 1899, 1902, 1903)
2: Hélène Prévost (1900)
3: P. Girod (1901)
4: Kate Gillou (then wed. Fenwick) (1904, 1905, 1906, 1908)
5: Countess Thérèse de Kermel (1907)
6: Jeanne Matthey (1909, 1910, 1911, 1912)
7: Marguerite Broquedis (1913, 1914)
8: Suzanne Lenglen (1920, 1921, 1922, 1923, 1925, 1926)
9: Julie Vlasto (1924)
10: Kornelia Bouman (1927)
11: Helen Wills (then wed. Moody) (1928, 1929, 1930, 1932)
12: Cilly Aussem (1931)
13: Margaret Scriven (1933, 1934)
14: Hilde Krahwinkel Sperling (1935, 1936, 1937)
15: Simonne Mathieu (1938, 1939)
16: Margaret Osborne (then wed. duPont) (1946, 1949)
17: Patricia Canning Todd (1947)
18: Nelly Adamson Landry (1948)
19: Doris Hart (1950, 1952)
20: Shirley Fry Irvin (1951) (tournament's Senior to this day)
21: Maureen Connolly (1953, 1954)
22: Angela Mortimer (1955)
23: Althea Gibson (1956)
24: Shirley Bloomer (1957)
25: Zsuzsa Kormoczy (1958)
26: Christine Truman (1959)
27: Darlene Hard (1960)
28: Ann Haydon-Jones (1961, 1966)
29: Margaret Smith (then wed. Court) (1962, 1964, 1969, 1970, 1973)
30: Lesley Turner (1963, 1965)
31: Françoise Durr (1967)
32: Nancy Richey (1968)
33: Evonne Goolagong (1971)
34: Billie Jean King (1972)
35: Chris Evert (then wed. Lloyd) (1974, 1975, 1979, 1980, 1983, 1985, 1986)
36: Sue Barker (1976)

37: Mima Jausovec (1977)
38: Virginia Ruzici (1978)
39: Hana Mandlikova (1981)
40: Martina Navratilova (1982, 1984)
41: Steffi Graf (1987, 1988, 1993, 1995, 1996, 1999)
42: Arantxa Sanchez Vicario (1989, 1994, 1998)
43: Monica Seles (1990, 1991, 1992)
44: Iva Majoli (1997)
45: Mary Pierce (2000)
46: Jennifer Capriati (2001)
47: Serena Williams (2002, 2013, 2015)
48: Justine Henin (2003, 2005, 2006, 2007)
49: Anastasia Myskina (2004)
50: Ana Ivanovic (2008)
51: Svetlana Kuznetsova (2009)
52: Francesca Schiavone (2010)
53: Li Na (2011)
54: Maria Sharapova (2012, 2014)

108 tournaments have been played.

Champions who were single at the time of their first victory have been listed under their maiden names. Their married names are quoted in brackets.

The tournament's senior is Shirley Fry Irvin, from the USA, 20th champion in 1951, born June 30, 1927 (88 years old).

ROLAND-GARROS

Men's Singles

French Championships

1891: H. Briggs def. M.P. Baigneres 6-3, 6-2
1892: Jean Schopfer def. Francis Louis Fassitt 6-2, 1-6, 6-2
1893: Laurent Riboulet def. Jean Schopfer 6-3, 6-3
1894: André Vacherot def. Gérard Brosselin 1-6, 6-3, 6-3
1895: André Vacherot def. Laurent Riboulet 9-7, 6-2
1896: André Vacherot def. Gérard Brosselin 6-1, 7-5
1897: Paul Aymé def. Francky Wardan 4-6, 6-4, 6-2
1898: Paul Aymé def. Paul Lebreton 5-7, 6-1, 6-2
1899: Paul Aymé def. Paul Lebreton 9-7, 3-6, 6-3
1900: Paul Aymé def. André Prévost 6-3, 6-0
1901: André Vacherot def. Paul Lebreton
1902: Michel Vacherot def. Max Decugis 6-4, 6-2
1903: Max Decugis def. André Vacherot 6-3, 6-2
1904: Max Decugis def. André Vacherot 6-1, 9-7, 6-8, 6-1
1905: Maurice Germot def. André Vacherot
1906: Maurice Germot def. Max Decugis 5-7, 6-3, 6-4, 1-6, 6-3
1907: Max Decugis def. Robert Wallet
1908: Max Decugis def. Maurice Germot 6-2, 6-1, 3-6, 10-8
1909: Max Decugis def. Maurice Germot 3-6, 2-6, 6-4, 6-4, 6-4
1910: Maurice Germot def. François Blanchy 6-1, 6-3, 4-6, 6-3
1911: André Gobert def. François Blanchy 6-1, 8-6, 7-5
1912: Max Decugis def. André Gobert
1913: Max Decugis def. Georges Gault 6-1, 6-3, 6-4
1914: Max Decugis def. Jean Samazeuilh 3-6, 6-1, 6-4, 6-4
1915 to 1919: no competition (due to WWI)
1920: André Gobert def. Max Decugis 6-3, 3-6, 1-6, 6-2, 6-3
1921: Jean Samazeuilh def. André Gobert 6-3, 6-3, 2-6, 7-5
1922: Henri Cochet def. Jean Samazeuilh 8-6, 6-3, 7-5
1923: François Blanchy def. Max Decugis 1-6, 6-2, 6-0, 6-2
1924: Jean Borotra def. René Lacoste 7-5, 6-4, 0-6, 5-7, 6-2

International French Championships

1925: René Lacoste def. Jean Borotra 7-5, 6-1, 6-4
1926: Henri Cochet def. René Lacoste 6-2, 6-4, 6-3
1927: René Lacoste def. William Tilden 6-4, 4-6, 5-7, 6-3, 11-9
1928: Henri Cochet def. René Lacoste 5-7, 6-3, 6-1, 6-3 **(First year at Roland-Garros Stadium)**
1929: René Lacoste def. Jean Borotra 6-3, 2-6, 6-0, 2-6, 8-6
1930: Henri Cochet def. William Tilden 3-6, 8-6, 6-3, 6-1
1931: Jean Borotra def. Christian Boussus 2-6, 6-4, 7-5, 6-4
1932: Henri Cochet def. Giorgio De Stefani 6-0, 6-4, 4-6, 6-3
1933: Jack Crawford def. Henri Cochet 8-6, 6-1, 6-3
1934: Gottfried von Cramm def. Jack Crawford 6-4, 7-9, 3-6, 7-5, 6-3
1935: Fred Perry def. Gottfried von Cramm 6-3, 3-6, 6-1, 6-3
1936: Gottfried von Cramm def. Fred Perry 6-0, 2-6, 6-2, 2-6, 6-0
1937: Henner Henkel def. Henry Austin 6-1, 6-4, 6-3
1938: Donald Budge def. Roderick Menzel 6-3, 6-2, 6-4
1939: William McNeill def. Bobby Riggs 7-5, 6-0, 6-3
1940 to 1945: no competition (due to WWII)
1946: Marcel Bernard def. Jaroslav Drobny 3-6, 2-6, 6-1, 6-4, 6-3
1947: Jozsef Asboth def. Erik Sturgess 8-6, 7-5, 6-4
1948: Frank Parker def. Jaroslav Drobny 6-4, 7-5, 5-7, 8-6
1949: Frank Parker def. Budge Patty 6-3, 1-6, 6-1, 6-4
1950: Budge Patty def. Jaroslav Drobny 6-1, 6-2, 3-6, 5-7, 7-5
1951: Jaroslav Drobny def. Erik Sturgess 6-3, 6-3, 6-3
1952: Jaroslav Drobny def. Frank Sedgman 6-2, 6-0, 3-6, 6-4
1953: Ken Rosewall def. Vic Seixas 6-3, 6-4, 1-6, 6-2
1954: Tony Trabert def. Arthur Larsen 6-4, 7-5, 6-1
1955: Tony Trabert def. Sven Davidson 2-6, 6-1, 6-4, 6-2
1956: Lewis Hoad def. Sven Davidson 6-4, 8-6, 6-3
1957: Sven Davidson def. Herbert Flam 6-3, 6-4, 6-4
1958: Mervyn Rose def. Luis Ayala 6-3, 6-4, 6-4
1959: Nicola Pietrangeli def. Ian Vermaak 3-6, 6-3, 6-4 6-1
1960: Nicola Pietrangeli def. Luis Ayala 3-6, 6-3, 6-4, 4-6, 6-3
1961: Manuel Santana def. Nicola Pietrangeli 4-6, 6-1, 3-6, 6-0, 6-2
1962: Rod Laver def. Roy Emerson 3-6, 2-6, 6-3, 9-7, 6-2
1963: Roy Emerson def. Pierre Darmon 3-6, 6-1, 6-4, 6-4
1964: Manuel Santana def. Nicola Pietrangeli 6-3, 6-1, 4-6, 7-5

1965: Fred Stolle def. Tony Roche 3-6, 6-0, 6-2, 6-3
1966: Tony Roche def. Istvan Gulyas 6-1, 6-4, 7-5
1967: Roy Emerson def. Tony Roche 6-1, 6-4, 2-6, 6-2

Open Era

1968: Ken Rosewall def. Rod Laver 6-3, 6-1, 2-6, 6-2
1969: Rod Laver def. Ken Rosewall 6-4, 6-3, 6-4
1970: Jan Kodes def. Zeljko Franulovic 6-2, 6-4, 6-0
1971: Jan Kodes def. Ilie Nastase 8-6, 6-2, 2-6, 7-5
1972: Andres Gimeno def. Patrick Proisy 4-6, 6-3, 6-1, 6-1
1973: Ilie Nastase def. Nikola Pilic 6-3, 6-3, 6-0
1974: Björn Borg def. Manuel Orantes 2-6, 6-7^1, 6-0, 6-1, 6-1
1975: Björn Borg def. Guillermo Vilas 6-2, 6-3, 6-4
1976: Adriano Panatta def. Harold Solomon 6-1, 6-4, 4-6, 7-6^3
1977: Guillermo Vilas def. Brian Gottfried 6-0, 6-3, 6-0
1978: Björn Borg def. Guillermo Vilas 6-1, 6-1, 6-3
1979: Björn Borg def. Victor Pecci 6-3, 6-1, 6-7^6, 6-4
1980: Björn Borg def. Vitas Gerulaitis 6-4, 6-1, 6-2
1981: Björn Borg def. Ivan Lendl 6-1, 4-6, 6-2, 3-6, 6-1
1982: Mats Wilander def. Guillermo Vilas 1-6, 7-6^6, 6-0, 6-4
1983: Yannick Noah def. Mats Wilander 6-2, 7-5, 7-6^3
1984: Ivan Lendl def. John McEnroe 3-6, 2-6, 6-4, 7-5, 7-5
1985: Mats Wilander def. Ivan Lendl 3-6, 6-4, 6-2, 6-2
1986: Ivan Lendl def. Mikael Pernfors 6-3, 6-2, 6-4
1987: Ivan Lendl def. Mats Wilander 7-5, 6-2, 3-6, 7-6^3
1988: Mats Wilander def. Henri Leconte 7-5, 6-2, 6-1
1989: Michael Chang def. Stefan Edberg 6-1, 3-6, 4-6, 6-4, 6-2
1990: Andres Gomez def. Andre Agassi 6-3, 2-6, 6-4, 6-4
1991: Jim Courier def. Andre Agassi 3-6, 6-4, 2-6, 6-1, 6-4
1992: Jim Courier def. Petr Korda 7-5, 6-2, 6-1
1993: Sergi Bruguera def. Jim Courier 6-4, 2-6, 6-2, 3-6, 6-3
1994: Sergi Bruguera def. Alberto Berasategui 6-3, 7-5, 2-6, 6-1
1995: Thomas Muster def. Michael Chang 7-5, 6-2, 6-4
1996: Yevgeny Kafelnikov def. Michael Stich 7-6^4, 7-5, 7-6^4
1997: Gustavo Kuerten def. Sergi Bruguera 6-3, 6-4, 6-2
1998: Carlos Moya def. Alex Corretja 6-3, 7-5, 6-3
1999: Andre Agassi def. Andrei Medvedev 1-6, 2-6, 6-4, 6-3, 6-4

2000: Gustavo Kuerten def. Magnus Norman 6-2, 6-3, 2-6, 7-6^6
2001: Gustavo Kuerten def. Alex Corretja 6-7^3, 7-5, 6-2, 6-0
2002: Albert Costa def. Juan Carlos Ferrero 6-1, 6-0, 4-6, 6-3
2003: Juan Carlos Ferrero def. Martin Verkerk 6-1, 6-3, 6-2
2004: Gaston Gaudio def. Guillermo Coria 0-6, 3-6, 6-4, 6-1, 8-6
2005: Rafael Nadal def. Mariano Puerta 6-7^6, 6-3, 6-1, 7-5
2006: Rafael Nadal def. Roger Federer 1-6, 6-1, 6-4, 7-6^4
2007: Rafael Nadal def. Roger Federer 6-3, 4-6, 6-3, 6-4
2008: Rafael Nadal def. Roger Federer 6-1, 6-3, 6-0
2009: Roger Federer def. Robin Söderling 6-1, 7-6^1, 6-4
2010: Rafael Nadal def. Robin Söderling 6-4, 6-2, 6-4
2011: Rafael Nadal def. Roger Federer 7-5, 7-6^3, 5-7, 6-1
2012: Rafael Nadal def. Novak Djokovic 6-4, 6-3, 2-6, 7-5
2013: Rafael Nadal def. David Ferrer 6-3, 6-2, 6-3
2014: Rafael Nadal def. Novak Djokovic 3-6, 7-5, 6-2, 6-4
2015: Stanislas Wawrinka def. Novak Djokovic 4-6, 6-4, 6-3, 6-4

All winners

1: H. Briggs (1891)
2: Jean Schopfer (1892)
3: Laurent Riboulet (1893)
4: André Vacherot (1894, 1895, 1896, 1901)
5: Paul Aymé (1897, 1898, 1899, 1900)
6: Michel Vacherot (1902)
7: Max Decugis (1903, 1904, 1907, 1908, 1909, 1912, 1913, 1914)
8: Maurice Germot (1905, 1906, 1910)
9: André Gobert (1911, 1920)
10: Jean Samazeuilh (1921)
11: Henri Cochet (1922, 1926, 1928, 1930, 1932)
12: François Blanchy (1923)
13: Jean Borotra (1924, 1931)
14: René Lacoste (1925, 1927, 1929)
15: Jack Crawford (1933)
16: Gottfried von Cramm (1934, 1936)
17: Fred Perry (1935)
18: Henner Henkel (1937)
19: Donald Budge (1938)
20: William McNeill (1939)
21: Marcel Bernard (1946)
22: Jozsef Asboth (1947)
23: Frank Parker (1948, 1949)
24: Budge Patty (1950) (tournament's Senior to this day)
25: Jaroslav Drobny (1951, 1952)
26: Ken Rosewall (1953, 1968)
27: Tony Trabert (1954, 1955)
28: Lewis Hoad (1956)
29: Sven Davidson (1957)
30: Mervyn Rose (1958)
31: Nicola Pietrangeli (1959, 1960)
32: Manuel Santana (1961, 1964)
33: Rod Laver (1962, 1969)
34: Roy Emerson (1963, 1967)
35: Fred Stolle (1965)
36: Tony Roche (1966)

37: Jan Kodes (1970, 1971)
38: Andres Gimeno (1972)
39: Ilie Nastase (1973)
40: Björn Borg (1974, 1975, 1978, 1979, 1980, 1981)
41: Adriano Panatta (1976)
42: Guillermo Vilas (1977)
43: Mats Wilander (1982, 1985, 1988)
44: Yannick Noah (1983)
45: Ivan Lendl (1984, 1986, 1987)
46: Michael Chang (1989)
47: Andres Gomez (1990)
48: Jim Courier (1991, 1992)
49: Sergi Bruguera (1993, 1994)
50: Thomas Muster (1995)
51: Yevgeny Kafelnikov (1996)
52: Gustavo Kuerten (1997, 2000, 2001)
53: Carlos Moya (1998)
54: Andre Agassi (1999)
55: Albert Costa (2002)
56: Juan Carlos Ferrero (2003)
57: Gaston Gaudio (2004)
58: Rafael Nadal (2005, 2006, 2007, 2008, 2010, 2011, 2012, 2013, 2014)
59: Roger Federer (2009)
60: Stanislas Wawrinka (2015)

114 tournaments have been played.

The tournament's senior is Budge Patty, from the USA, 24th champion in 1950, born February 11, 1924 (91 years old).

WIMBLEDON

Ladies' Singles

1884: Maud Watson def. Lillian Watson 6-8, 6-3, 6-3
1885: Maud Watson def. Blanche Bingley 6-1, 7-5
1886: Blanche Bingley def. Maud Watson 6-3, 6-3
1887: Lottie Dod def. Blanche Bingley 6-2, 6-0
1888: Lottie Dod def. Blanche Bingley Hillyard 6-3, 6-3
1889: Blanche Bingley Hillyard def. Lena Rice 4-6, 8-6, 6-4
1890: Lena Rice def. May Jacks 6-4, 6-1
1891: Lottie Dod def. Blanche Bingley Hillyard 6-2, 6-1
1892: Lottie Dod def. Blanche Bingley Hillyard 6-1, 6-1
1893: Lottie Dod def. Blanche Bingley Hillyard 6-8, 6-1, 6-4
1894: Blanche Bingley Hillyard def. Edith Austin 6-1, 6-1
1895: Charlotte Cooper Sterry def. Helen Jackson 7-5, 7-6
1896: Charlotte Cooper Sterry def. Alice Simpson Pickering 6-2, 6-3
1897: Blanche Bingley Hillyard def. Charlotte Cooper Sterry 5-7, 7-5, 6-2
1898: Charlotte Cooper Sterry def. Mary Louisa Martin 6-4, 6-4
1899: Blanche Bingley Hillyard def. Charlotte Cooper Sterry 6-2, 6-3
1900: Blanche Bingley Hillyard def. Charlotte Cooper Sterry 4-6, 6-4, 6-4
1901: Charlotte Cooper Sterry def. Blanche Bingley Hillyard 6-2, 6-2
1902: Muriel Robb def. Charlotte Cooper Sterry 7-5, 6-1
1903: Dorothea Douglass def. Ethel Thomson Larcombe 4-6, 6-4, 6-2
1904: Dorothea Douglass def. Charlotte Cooper Sterry 6-0, 6-3
1905: May Sutton Bundy def. Dorothea Douglass 6-3, 6-4
1906: Dorothea Douglass def. May Sutton Bundy 6-3, 9-7
1907: May Sutton Bundy def. Dorothea Lambert-Chambers 6-1, 6-4
1908: Charlotte Cooper Sterry def. Agnes Morton 6-4, 6-4
1909: Dora Boothby def. Agnes Morton 6-4, 4-6, 8-6
1910: Dorothea Lambert-Chambers def. Dora Boothby 6-2, 6-2
1911: Dorothea Lambert-Chambers def. Dora Boothby 6-0, 6-0
1912: Ethel Thomson Larcombe def. Charlotte Cooper Sterry 6-3, 6-1
1913: Dorothea Lambert-Chambers def. Winifred McNair 6-0, 6-4
1914: Dorothea Lambert-Chambers def. Ethel Thomson Larcombe 7-5, 6-4
1915 to 1918: no competition (due to WWI)
1919: Suzanne Lenglen def. Dorothea Lambert-Chambers 10-8, 4-6, 9-7

1920: Suzanne Lenglen def. Dorothea Lambert-Chambers 6-3, 6-0
1921: Suzanne Lenglen def. Elizabeth Ryan 6-2, 6-0
1922: Suzanne Lenglen def. Molla Bjurstedt Mallory 6-2, 6-0
1923: Suzanne Lenglen def. Kathleen McKane Godfree 6-2, 6-2
1924: Kathleen McKane Godfree def. Helen Wills 4-6, 6-4, 6-4
1925: Suzanne Lenglen def. Joan Fry 6-2, 6-0
1926: Kathleen McKane Godfree def. Lili Alvarez 6-2, 4-6, 6-3
1927: Helen Wills def. Lili Alvarez 6-2, 6-4
1928: Helen Wills def. Lili Alvarez 6-2, 6-3
1929: Helen Wills def. Helen Hull Jacobs 6-1, 6-2
1930: Helen Wills Moody def. Elizabeth Ryan 6-2, 6-2
1931: Cilly Aussem def. Hilde Krahwinkel Sperling 6-2, 7-5
1932: Helen Wills Moody def. Helen Hull Jacobs 6-3, 6-1
1933: Helen Wills Moody def. Dorothy Round Little 6-4, 6-8, 6-3
1934: Dorothy Round Little def. Helen Hull Jacobs 6-2, 5-7, 6-3
1935: Helen Wills Moody def. Helen Hull Jacobs 6-3, 3-6, 7-5
1936: Helen Hull Jacobs def. Hilde Krahwinkel Sperling 6-2, 4-6, 7-5
1937: Dorothy Round Little def. Jadwiga Jedrzejowska 6-2, 2-6, 7-5
1938: Helen Wills Moody def. Helen Hull Jacobs 6-4, 6-0
1939: Alice Marble def. Kay Stammers 6-2, 6-0
1940 to 1945: no competition (due to WWII)
1946: Pauline Betz Addie def. Louise Brough Clapp 6-2, 6-4
1947: Margaret Osborne def. Doris Hart 6-2, 6-4
1948: Louise Brough Clapp def. Doris Hart 6-3, 8-6
1949: Louise Brough Clapp def. Margaret Osborne duPont 10-8, 1-6, 10-8
1950: Louise Brough Clapp def. Margaret Osborne duPont 6-1, 3-6, 6-1
1951: Doris Hart def. Shirley Fry Irvin 6-1, 6-0
1952: Maureen Connolly def. Louise Brough Clapp 7-5, 6-3
1953: Maureen Connolly def. Doris Hart 8-6, 7-5
1954: Maureen Connolly def. Louise Brough Clapp 6-2, 7-5
1955: Louise Brough Clapp def. Beverly Baker Fleitz 7-5, 8-6
1956: Shirley Fry Irvin def. Angela Buxton 6-3, 6-1
1957: Althea Gibson def. Darlene Hard 6-3, 6-2
1958: Althea Gibson def. Angela Mortimer 8-6, 6-2
1959: Maria Bueno def. Darlene Hard 6-4, 6-3
1960: Maria Bueno def. Sandra Reynolds Price 8-6, 6-0
1961: Angela Mortimer def. Christine Truman 4-6, 6-4, 7-5
1962: Karen Hantze Susman def. Vera Sukova 6-4, 6-4

1963: Margaret Smith def. Billie Jean Moffitt 6-3, 6-4
1964: Maria Bueno def. Margaret Smith 6-4, 7-9, 6-3
1965: Margaret Smith def. Maria Bueno 6-4, 7-5
1966: Billie Jean King def. Maria Bueno 6-3, 3-6, 6-1
1967: Billie Jean King def. Ann Haydon-Jones 6-3, 6-4

Open Era

1968: Billie Jean King def. Judy Tegart-Dalton 9-7, 7-5
1969: Ann Haydon-Jones def. Billie Jean King 3-6, 6-3, 6-2
1970: Margaret Smith Court def. Billie Jean King 14-12, 11-9
1971: Evonne Goolagong def. Margaret Smith Court 6-4, 6-1
1972: Billie Jean King def. Evonne Goolagong 6-3, 6-3
1973: Billie Jean King def. Chris Evert 6-0, 7-5
1974: Chris Evert def. Olga Morozova 6-0, 6-4
1975: Billie Jean King def. Evonne Goolagong-Cawley 6-0, 6-1
1976: Chris Evert def. Evonne Goolagong-Cawley 6-3, 4-6, 8-6
1977: Virginia Wade def. Betty Stove 4-6, 6-3, 6-1
1978: Martina Navratilova def. Chris Evert 2-6, 6-4, 7-5
1979: Martina Navratilova def. Chris Evert-Lloyd 6-4, 6-4
1980: Evonne Goolagong-Cawley def. Chris Evert-Lloyd 6-1, 7-6^4
1981: Chris Evert-Lloyd def. Hana Mandlikova 6-2, 6-2
1982: Martina Navratilova def. Chris Evert-Lloyd 6-1, 3-6, 6-2
1983: Martina Navratilova def. Andrea Jaeger 6-0, 6-3
1984: Martina Navratilova def. Chris Evert-Lloyd 7-6^5, 6-2
1985: Martina Navratilova def. Chris Evert-Lloyd 4-6, 6-3, 6-2
1986: Martina Navratilova def. Hana Mandlikova 7-6^1, 6-3
1987: Martina Navratilova def. Steffi Graf 7-5, 6-3
1988: Steffi Graf def. Martina Navratilova 5-7, 6-2, 6-1
1989: Steffi Graf def. Martina Navratilova 6-2, 6-7^1, 6-1
1990: Martina Navratilova def. Zina Garrison 6-4, 6-1
1991: Steffi Graf def. Gabriela Sabatini 6-4, 3-6, 8-6
1992: Steffi Graf def. Monica Seles 6-2, 6-1
1993: Steffi Graf def. Jana Novotna 7-6^6, 1-6, 6-4
1994: Conchita Martinez def. Martina Navratilova 6-4, 3-6, 6-3
1995: Steffi Graf def. Arantxa Sanchez Vicario 4-6, 6-1, 7-5
1996: Steffi Graf def. Arantxa Sanchez Vicario 6-3, 7-5
1997: Martina Hingis def. Jana Novotna 2-6, 6-3, 6-3

1998: Jana Novotna def. Nathalie Tauziat 6-4, 7-6^2
1999: Lindsay Davenport def. Steffi Graf 6-4, 7-5
2000: Venus Williams def. Lindsay Davenport 6-3, 7-6^3
2001: Venus Williams def. Justine Henin 6-1, 3-6, 6-0
2002: Serena Williams def. Venus Williams 7-6^4, 6-3
2003: Serena Williams def. Venus Williams 4-6, 6-4, 6-2
2004: Maria Sharapova def. Serena Williams 6-1, 6-4
2005: Venus Williams def. Lindsay Davenport Leach 4-6, 7-6^4, 9-7
2006: Amélie Mauresmo def. Justine Henin-Hardenne 2-6, 6-3, 6-4
2007: Venus Williams def. Marion Bartoli 6-4, 6-1
2008: Venus Williams def. Serena Williams 7-5, 6-4
2009: Serena Williams def. Venus Williams 7-6^3, 6-2
2010: Serena Williams def. Vera Zvonareva 6-3, 6-2
2011: Petra Kvitova def. Maria Sharapova 6-3, 6-4
2012: Serena Williams def. Agnieska Radwanska 6-1, 5-7, 6-2
2013: Marion Bartoli def. Sabine Lisicki 6-1, 6-4
2014: Petra Kvitova def. Eugénie Bouchard 6-3, 6-0
2015: Serena Williams def. Garbine Muguruza 6-4, 6-4

The challenge round was played at Wimbledon from 1886 until 1921; the defending champion was automatically qualified for the final (without playing any other match). All other players were engaged in the tournament and the finalist was then opposed to the previous year's champion. The current year's champion was the winner of that "second" final. When the defending champion forfeited, the tournament's new champion was the winner of the single elimination phase. This happened in 1889, 1890, 1891, 1894, 1895, 1898, 1903, 1908, 1909, 1912 and 1913.

All winners

1: Maud Watson (1884, 1885)
2: Blanche Bingley (then wed. Hillyard) (1886, 1889, 1894, 1897, 1899, 1900)
3: Lottie Dod (1887, 1888, 1891, 1892, 1893)
4: Lena Rice (1890)
5: Charlotte Cooper Sterry (1895, 1896, 1898, 1901, 1908)
6: Muriel Robb (1902)
7: Dorothea Douglass (then wed. Lambert-Chambers) (1903, 1904, 1906, 1910, 1911, 1913, 1914)
8: May Sutton Bundy (1905, 1907)
9: Dora Boothby (1909)
10: Ethel Thomson Larcombe (1912)
11: Suzanne Lenglen (1919, 1920, 1921, 1922, 1923, 1925)
12: Kathleen McKane Godfree (1924, 1926)
13: Helen Wills (then wed. Moody) (1927, 1928, 1929, 1930, 1932, 1933, 1935, 1938)
14: Cilly Aussem (1931)
15: Dorothy Round Little (1934, 1937)
16: Helen Hull Jacobs (1936)
17: Alice Marble (1939)
18: Pauline Betz Addie (1946)
19: Margaret Osborne (1947)
20: Louise Brough Clapp (1948, 1949, 1950, 1955)
21: Doris Hart (1951)
22: Maureen Connolly (1952, 1953, 1954)
23: **Shirley Fry Irvin (1956) (tournament's Senior to this day)**
24: Althea Gibson (1957, 1958)
25: Maria Bueno (1959, 1960, 1964)
26: Angela Mortimer (1961)
27: Karen Hantze Susman (1962)
28: Margaret Smith (then wed. Court) (1963, 1965, 1970)
29: Billie Jean King (1966, 1967, 1968, 1972, 1973, 1975)
30: Ann Haydon-Jones (1969)
31: Evonne Goolagong (then wed. Cawley) (1971, 1980)
32: Chris Evert (then wed. Lloyd) (1974, 1976, 1981)
33: Virginia Wade (1977)
34: Martina Navratilova (1978, 1979, 1982, 1983, 1984, 1985, 1986, 1987, 1990)
35: Steffi Graf (1988, 1989, 1991, 1992, 1993, 1995, 1996)
36: Conchita Martinez (1994)

37: Martina Hingis (1997)
38: Jana Novotna (1998)
39: Lindsay Davenport (1999)
40: Venus Williams (2000, 2001, 2005, 2007, 2008)
41: Serena Williams (2002, 2003, 2009, 2010, 2012, 2015)
42: Maria Sharapova (2004)
43: Amélie Mauresmo (2006)
44: Petra Kvitova (2011, 2014)
45: Marion Bartoli (2013)

122 tournaments have been played.

Champions who were single at the time of their first victory have been listed under their maiden names. Their married names are quoted in brackets.

The tournament's senior is Shirley Fry Irvin, from the USA, 23rd champion in 1956, born June 30, 1927 (88 years old).

WIMBLEDON

Gentlemen's Singles

1877: Spencer Gore def. William Marshall 6-1, 6-2, 6-4
1878: Frank Hadow def. Spencer Gore 7-5, 6-1, 9-7
1879: John Hartley def. Frank Hadow, walkover
    1879: John Hartley def. Vere St. Leger Goold 6-2, 6-4, 6-2
1880: John Hartley def. Herbert Lawford 6-0, 6-2, 2-6, 6-3
1881: William Renshaw def. John Hartley 6-0, 6-2, 6-1
1882: William Renshaw def. Ernest Renshaw 6-1, 2-6, 4-6, 6-2, 6-2
1883: William Renshaw def. Ernest Renshaw 2-6, 6-3, 6-3, 4-6, 6-3
1884: William Renshaw def. Herbert Lawford 6-0, 6-4, 9-7
1885: William Renshaw def. Herbert Lawford 7-5, 6-2, 4-6, 7-5
1886: William Renshaw def. Herbert Lawford 6-0, 5-7, 6-3, 6-4
1887: Herbert Lawford def. Willliam Renshaw, walkover
    1887: Herbert Lawford def. Ernest Renshaw 1-6, 6-3, 3-6, 6-4, 6-4
1888: Ernest Renshaw def. Herbert Lawford 6-3, 7-5, 6-0
1889: William Renshaw def. Ernest Renshaw 6-4, 6-1, 3-6, 6-0
1890: Willoughby Hamilton def. William Renshaw 6-8, 6-2, 3-6, 6-1, 6-1
1891: Wilfred Baddeley def. Willoughby Hamilton, walkover
    1891: Wilfred Baddeley def. Joshua Pim 6-4, 1-6, 7-5, 6-0
1892: Wilfred Baddeley def. Joshua Pim 4-6, 6-3, 6-3, 6-2
1893: Joshua Pim def. Wilfred Baddeley 3-6, 6-1, 6-3, 6-2
1894: Joshua Pim def. Wilfred Baddeley 10-8, 6-2, 8-6
1895: Wilfred Baddeley def. Joshua Pim, walkover
    1895: Wilfred Baddeley def. Wilberforce Eaves 4-6, 2-6, 8-6, 6-2, 6-3
1896: Harold Mahony def. Wilfred Baddeley 6-2, 6-8, 5-7, 8-6, 6-3
1897: Reggie Doherty def. Harold Mahony 6-4, 6-4, 6-3
1898: Reggie Doherty def. Laurie Doherty 6-3, 6-3, 2-6, 5-7, 6-1
1899: Reggie Doherty def. Arthur Gore 1-6, 4-6, 6-2, 6-3, 6-3
1900: Reggie Doherty def. Sidney Smith 6-8, 6-3, 6-1, 6-2
1901: Arthur Gore def. Reggie Doherty 4-6, 7-5, 6-4, 6-4
1902: Laurie Doherty def. Arthur Gore 6-4, 6-3, 3-6, 6-0
1903: Laurie Doherty def. Frank Riseley 7-5, 6-3, 6-0
1904: Laurie Doherty def. Frank Riseley 6-1, 7-5, 8-6
1905: Laurie Doherty def. Norman Brookes 8-6, 6-2, 6-4

1906: Laurie Doherty def. Frank Riseley 6-4, 4-6, 6-2, 6-3
1907: Norman Brookes def. Laurie Doherty, walkover
  1907: Norman Brookes def. Arthur Gore 6-4, 6-2, 6-2
1908: Arthur Gore def. Norman Brookes, walkover
  1908: Arthur Gore def. Herbert Roper Barrett 6-3, 6-2, 4-6, 3-6, 6-4
1909: Arthur Gore def. Josiah Ritchie 6-8, 1-6, 6-2, 6-2, 6-2
1910: Tony Wilding def. Arthur Gore 6-4, 7-5, 4-6, 6-2
1911: Tony Wilding def. Herbert Roper Barrett 6-4, 4-6, 2-6, 6-2, ret.
1912: Tony Wilding def. Arthur Gore 6-4, 6-4, 4-6, 6-4
1913: Tony Wilding def. Maurice McLoughlin 8-6, 6-3, 10-8
1914: Norman Brookes def. Tony Wilding 6-4, 6-4, 7-5
1915 to 1918: no competition (due to WWI)
1919: Gerald Patterson def. Norman Brookes 6-3, 7-5, 6-2
1920: Willliam Tilden def. Gerald Patterson 2-6, 6-3, 6-2, 6-4
1921: William Tilden def. Brian Norton 4-6, 2-6, 6-1, 6-0, 7-5
1922: Gerald Paterson def. Randolph Lycett 6-3, 6-4, 6-2
1923: Bill Johnston def. Francis Hunter 6-0, 6-3, 6-1
1924: Jean Borotra def. René Lacoste 6-1, 3-6, 6-1, 3-6, 6-4
1925: René Lacoste def. Jean Borotra 6-3, 6-3, 4-6, 8-6
1926: Jean Borotra def. Howard Kinsey 8-6, 6-1, 6-3
1927: Henri Cochet def. Jean Borotra 4-6, 4-6, 6-3, 6-4, 7-5
1928: René Lacoste def. Henri Cochet 6-1, 4-6, 6-4, 6-2
1929: Henri Cochet def. Jean Borotra 6-4, 6-3, 6-4
1930: William Tilden def. Wilmer Allison 6-3, 9-7, 6-4
1931: Sidney Wood def. Frank Shields, walkover
1932: Ellsworth Vines def. Henry Austin 6-4, 6-2, 6-0
1933: Jack Crawford def. Ellsworth Vines 4-6 11-9 6-2 2-6 6-4
1934: Fred Perry def. Jack Crawford 6-3 6-0 7-5
1935: Fred Perry def. Gottfried von Cramm 6-2 6-4 6-4
1936: Fred Perry def. Gottfried von Cramm 6-1, 6-1, 6-0
1937: Donald Budge def. Gottfried von Cramm 6-3, 6-4, 6-2
1938: Donald Budge def. Henry Austin 6-1, 6-0, 6-3
1939: Bobby Riggs def. Elwood Cooke 2-6, 8-6, 3-6, 6-3, 6-2
1940 to 1945: no competition (due to WWII)
1946: Yvon Petra def. Geoffrey Brown 6-2, 6-4, 7-9, 5-7, 6-4
1947: Jack Kramer def. Tom Brown 6-1, 6-3, 6-2
1948: Bob Falkenburg def. John Bromwich 7-5, 0-6, 6-2, 3-6, 7-5
1949: Ted Schroeder def. Jaroslav Drobny 3-6, 6-0, 6-3, 4-6, 6-4

1950: Budge Patty def. Frank Sedgman 6-1, 8-10, 6-2, 6-3
1951: Dick Savitt def. Ken McGregor 6-4, 6-4, 6-4
1952: Frank Sedgman def. Jaroslav Drobny 4-6, 6-2, 6-3, 6-2
1953: Vic Seixas def. Kurt Nielsen 9-7, 6-3, 6-4
1954: Jaroslav Drobny def. Ken Rosewall 13-11, 4-6, 6-2, 9-7
1955: Tony Trabert def. Kurt Nielsen 6-3, 7-5, 6-1
1956: Lewis Hoad def. Ken Rosewall 6-2, 4-6, 7-5, 6-4
1957: Lewis Hoad def. Ashley Cooper 6-2, 6-1, 6-2
1958: Ashley Cooper def. Neale Fraser 3-6, 6-3, 6-4, 13-11
1959: Alex Olmedo def. Rod Laver 6-4, 6-3, 6-4
1960: Neale Fraser def. Rod Laver 6-4, 3-6, 9-7, 7-5
1961: Rod Laver def. Chuck McKinley 6-3, 6-1, 6-4
1962: Rod Laver def. Martin Mulligan 6-2, 6-2, 6-1
1963: Chuck McKinley def. Fred Stolle 9-7, 6-1, 6-4
1964: Roy Emerson def. Fred Stolle 6-4, 12-10, 4-6, 6-3
1965: Roy Emerson def. Fred Stolle 6-2, 6-4, 6-4
1966: Manuel Santana def. Dennis Ralston 6-4, 11-9, 6-4
1967: John Newcombe def. Wilhelm Bungert 6-3, 6-1, 6-1

Open Era

1968: Rod Laver def. Tony Roche 6-3, 6-4, 6-2
1969: Rod Laver def. John Newcombe 6-4, 5-7, 6-4, 6-4
1970: John Newcombe def. Ken Rosewall 5-7, 6-3, 6-2, 3-6, 6-1
1971: John Newcombe def. Stan Smith 6-3, 5-7, 2-6, 6-4, 6-4
1972: Stan Smith def. Ilie Nastase 4-6, 6-3, 6-3, 4-6, 7-5
1973: Jan Kodes def. Alex Metreveli 6-1, 9-8[5], 6-3
1974: Jimmy Connors def. Ken Rosewall 6-1, 6-1, 6-4
1975: Arthur Ashe def. Jimmy Connors 6-1, 6-1, 5-7, 6-4
1976: Björn Borg def. Ilie Nastase 6-4, 6-2, 9-7
1977: Björn Borg def. Jimmy Connors 3-6, 6-2, 6-1, 5-7, 6-4
1978: Björn Borg def. Jimmy Connors 6-2, 6-2, 6-3
1979: Björn Borg def. Roscoe Tanner 6-7[4], 6-1, 3-6, 6-3, 6-4
1980: Björn Borg def. John McEnroe 1-6, 7-5, 6-3, 6-7[16], 8-6
1981: John McEnroe def. Björn Borg 4-6, 7-6[1], 7-6[4], 6-4
1982: Jimmy Connors def. John McEnroe 3-6, 6-3, 6-7[2], 7-6[5], 6-4
1983: John McEnroe def. Chris Lewis 6-2, 6-2, 6-2
1984: John McEnroe def. Jimmy Connors 6-1, 6-1, 6-2

1985: Boris Becker def. Kevin Curren 6-3, 6-7^4, 7-6^3, 6-4
1986: Boris Becker def. Ivan Lendl 6-4, 6-3, 7-5
1987: Pat Cash def. Ivan Lendl 7-6^5, 6-2, 7-5
1988: Stefan Edberg def. Boris Becker 4-6, 7-6^2, 6-4, 6-2
1989: Boris Becker def. Stefan Edberg 6-0, 7-6^1, 6-4
1990: Stefan Edberg def. Boris Becker 6-2, 6-2, 3-6, 3-6, 6-4
1991: Michael Stich def. Boris Becker 6-4, 7-6^4, 6-4
1992: Andre Agassi def. Goran Ivanisevic 6-7^8, 6-4, 6-4, 1-6, 6-4
1993: Pete Sampras def. Jim Courier 7-6^3, 7-6^6, 3-6, 6-3
1994: Pete Sampras def. Goran Ivanisevic 7-6^2, 7-6^5, 6-0
1995: Pete Sampras def. Boris Becker 6-7^5, 6-2, 6-4, 6-2
1996: Richard Krajicek def. MaliVai Washington 6-3, 6-4, 6-3
1997: Pete Sampras def. Cédric Pioline 6-4, 6-2, 6-4
1998: Pete Sampras def. Goran Ivanisevic 6-7^2, 7-6^9, 6-4, 3-6, 6-2
1999: Pete Sampras def. Andre Agassi 6-3, 6-4, 7-5
2000: Pete Sampras def. Patrick Rafter 6-7^{10}, 7-6^5, 6-4, 6-2
2001: Goran Ivanisevic def. Patrick Rafter 6-3, 3-6, 6-3, 2-6, 9-7
2002: Lleyton Hewitt def. David Nalbandian 6-2, 6-3, 6-2
2003: Roger Federer def. Mark Philippoussis 7-6^5, 6-3, 7-6^3
2004: Roger Federer def. Andy Roddick 4-6, 7-5, 7-6^3, 6-4
2005: Roger Federer def. Andy Roddick 6-2, 7-6^2, 6-4
2006: Roger Federer def. Rafael Nadal 6-0, 7-6^5, 6-7^2, 6-3
2007: Roger Federer def. Rafael Nadal 7-6^7, 4-6, 7-6^3, 2-6, 6-2
2008: Rafael Nadal def. Roger Federer 6-4, 6-4, 6-7^5, 6-7^8, 9-7
2009: Roger Federer def. Andy Roddick 5-7, 7-6^6, 7-6^5, 3-6, 16-14
2010: Rafael Nadal def. Tomas Berdych 6-3, 7-5, 6-4
2011: Novak Djokovic def. Rafael Nadal 6-4, 6-1, 1-6, 6-3
2012: Roger Federer def. Andy Murray 4-6, 7-5, 6-3, 6-4
2013: Andy Murray def. Novak Djokovic 6-4, 7-5, 6-4
2014: Novak Djokovic def. Roger Federer 6-7^7, 6-4, 7-6^4, 5-7, 6-4
2015: Novak Djokovic def. Roger Federer 7-6^1, 6-7^{10}, 6-4, 6-3

The challenge round was played at Wimbledon from 1878 until 1921; the defending champion was automatically qualified for the final (without playing any other match). All other players were engaged in the tournament and the finalist was then opposed to the previous year's champion. The current year's champion was the winner of that "second" final. When the defending champion forfeited, the tournament's new champion was the winner of the single elimination phase. This happened in 1879, 1887, 1891, 1895, 1907 and 1908.

All winners

1: Spencer Gore (1877)
2: Frank Hadow (1878)
3: John Hartley (1879, 1880)
4: William Renshaw (1881, 1882, 1883, 1884, 1885, 1886, 1889)
5: Herbert Lawford (1887)
6: Ernest Renshaw (1888)
7: Willoughby Hamilton (1890)
8: Wilfred Baddeley (1891, 1892, 1895)
9: Joshua Pim (1893, 1894)
10: Harold Mahony (1896)
11: Reggie Doherty (1897, 1898, 1899, 1900)
12: Arthur Gore (1901, 1908, 1909)
13: Laurie Doherty (1902, 1903, 1904, 1905, 1906)
14: Norman Brookes (1907, 1914)
15: Tony Wilding (1910, 1911, 1912, 1913)
16: Gerald Patterson (1919, 1922)
17: William Tilden (1920, 1921, 1930)
18: Bill Johnston (1923)
19: Jean Borotra (1924, 1926)
20: René Lacoste (1925, 1928)
21: Henri Cochet (1927, 1929)
22: Sidney Wood (1931)
23: Ellsworth Vines (1932)
24: Jack Crawford (1933)
25: Fred Perry (1934, 1935, 1936)
26: Donald Budge (1937, 1938)
27: Bobby Riggs (1939)
28: Yvon Petra (1946)
29: Jack Kramer (1947)
30: Bob Falkenburg (1948)
31: Ted Schroeder (1949)
32: Budge Patty (1950)
33: Dick Savitt (1951)
34: Frank Sedgman (1952)
35: Vic Seixas (1953) (tournament's Senior to this day)
36: Jaroslav Drobny (1954)

37: Tony Trabert (1955)
38: Lewis Hoad (1956, 1957)
39: Ashley Cooper (1958)
40: Alex Olmedo (1959)
41: Neale Fraser (1960)
42: Rod Laver (1961, 1962, 1968, 1969)
43: Chuck McKinley (1963)
44: Roy Emerson (1964, 1965)
45: Manuel Santana (1966)
46: John Newcombe (1967, 1970, 1971)
47: Stan Smith (1972)
48: Jan Kodes (1973)
49: Jimmy Connors (1974, 1982)
50 : Arthur Ashe (1975)
51: Björn Borg (1976, 1977, 1978, 1979, 1980)
52: John McEnroe (1981, 1983, 1984)
53: Boris Becker (1985, 1986, 1989)
54: Pat Cash (1987)
55: Stefan Edberg (1988, 1990)
56: Michael Stich (1991)
57: Andre Agassi (1992)
58: Pete Sampras (1993, 1994, 1995, 1997, 1998, 1999, 2000)
59: Richard Krajicek (1996)
60: Goran Ivanisevic (2001)
61: Lleyton Hewitt (2002)
62: Roger Federer (2003, 2004, 2005, 2006, 2007, 2009, 2012)
63: Rafael Nadal (2008, 2010)
64: Novak Djokovic (2011, 2014, 2015)
65: Andy Murray (2013)

129 tournaments have been played.

The tournament's senior is Vic Seixas, from the USA, 35th champion in 1953, born August 30, 1923 (92 years old).

US OPEN

Women's Singles

US Championships

1887: Ellen Hansell def. Laura Knight 6-1, 6-0
1888: Bertha Townsend def. Ellen Hansell 6-3, 6-5
1889: Bertha Townsend def. Lida Voorhees 7-5, 6-2
1890: Ellen Roosevelt def. Bertha Townsend 6-2, 6-2
1891: Mabel Cahill def. Ellen Roosevelt 6-4, 6-1, 4-6, 6-3
1892: Mabel Cahill def. Elisabeth Moore 5-7, 6-3, 6-4, 4-6, 6-2
1893: Aline Terry def. Augusta Schultz 6-1, 6-3
1894: Helen Hellwig def. Aline Terry 7-5, 3-6, 6-0, 3-6, 6-3
1895: Juliette Atkinson def. Helen Hellwig 6-4, 6-2, 6-1
1896: Elisabeth Moore def. Juliette Atkinson 6-4, 4-6, 6-2, 6-2
1897: Juliette Atkinson def. Elisabeth Moore 6-3, 6-3, 4-6, 3-6, 6-3
1898: Juliette Atkinson def. Marion Jones 6-3, 5-7, 6-4, 2-6, 7-5
1899: Marion Jones def. Maud Banks 6-1, 6-1, 7-5
1900: Myrtle McAteer def. Edith Parker 6-2, 6-2, 6-0
1901: Elisabeth Moore def. Myrtle McAteer 6-4, 3-6, 7-5, 2-6, 6-2
1902: Marion Jones def. Elisabeth Moore 6-1, 1-0, ret.
1903: Elisabeth Moore def. Marion Jones Farquhar 7-5, 8-6
1904: May Sutton Bundy def. Elisabeth Moore 6-1, 6-2
1905: Elisabeth Moore def. Helen Homans 6-4, 5-7, 6-1
1906: Helen Homans def. Maud Barger Wallach 6-2, 6-3
1907: Evelyn Sears def. Carrie Neely 6-3, 6-2
1908: Maud Barger Wallach def. Evelyn Sears 6-3, 1-6, 6-3
1909: Hazel Hotchkiss def. Maud Barger Wallach 6-0, 6-1
1910: Hazel Hotchkiss def. Louise Hammond 6-4, 6-2
1911: Hazel Hotchkiss def. Florence Sutton 8-10, 6-1, 9-7
1912: Mary Kendall Browne def. Eleonora Sears 6-4, 6-2
1913: Mary Kendall Browne def. Dorothy Green 6-2, 7-5
1914: Mary Kendall Browne def. Marie Wagner 6-2, 1-6, 6-1
1915: Molla Bjurstedt Mallory def. Hazel Hotchkiss Wightman 4-6, 6-2, 6-0
1916: Molla Bjurstedt Mallory def. Louise Hammond 6-0, 6-1
1917: Molla Bjurstedt Mallory def. Marion Vanderhoef 4-6, 6-0, 6-2

1918: Molla Bjurstedt Mallory def. Eleanor Goss 6-4, 6-3
1919: Hazel Hotchkiss Wightman def. Marion Zinderstein 6-1, 6-2
1920: Molla Bjurstedt Mallory def. Marion Zinderstein 6-3, 6-1
1921: Molla Bjurstedt Mallory def. Mary Kendall Browne 4-6, 6-4, 6-2
1922: Molla Bjurstedt Mallory def. Helen Wills 6-3, 6-1
1923: Helen Wills def. Molla Bjurstedt Mallory 6-2, 6-1
1924: Helen Wills def. Molla Bjurstedt Mallory 6-1, 6-3
1925: Helen Wills def. Kathleen McKane Godfree 3-6, 6-0, 6-2
1926: Molla Bjurstedt Mallory def. Elizabeth Ryan 4-6, 6-4, 9-7
1927: Helen Wills def. Betty Nuthall 6-1, 6-4
1928: Helen Wills def. Helen Hull Jacobs 6-2, 6-1
1929: Helen Wills def. Phoebe Holcroft Watson 6-2, 6-1
1930: Betty Nuthall def. Anna McCune Harper 6-1, 6-4
1931: Helen Wills Moody def. Eileen Bennett Fearnley Whittingstall 6-4, 6-1
1932: Helen Hull Jacobs def. Carolin Babcock Stark 6-2, 6-2
1933: Helen Hull Jacobs def. Helen Wills Moody 8-6, 3-6, 3-0, ret.
1934: Helen Hull Jacobs def. Sarah Palfrey 6-1, 6-4
1935: Helen Hull Jacobs def. Sarah Palfrey Fabyan 6-2, 6-4
1936: Alice Marble def. Helen Hull Jacobs 4-6, 6-3, 6-2
1937: Anita Lizana def. Jadwiga Jedrzejowska 6-4, 6-2
1938: Alice Marble def. Nancye Wynne Bolton 6-0, 6-3
1939: Alice Marble def. Helen Hull Jacobs 6-0, 8-10, 6-4
1940: Alice Marble def. Helen Hull Jacobs 6-2, 6-3
1941: Sarah Palfrey Cooke def. Pauline Betz Addie 7-5, 6-2
1942: Pauline Betz Addie def. Louise Brough Clapp 4-6, 6-1, 6-4
1943: Pauline Betz Addie def. Louise Brough Clapp 6-3, 5-7, 6-3
1944: Pauline Betz Addie def. Margaret Osborne 6-3, 8-6
1945: Sarah Palfrey Cooke def. Pauline Betz Addie 3-6, 8-6, 6-4
1946: Pauline Betz Addie def. Patricia Canning Todd 11-9, 6-3
1947: Louise Brough Clapp def. Margaret Osborne 6-3, 8-6
1948: Margaret Osborne duPont def. Louise Brough Clapp 4-6, 6-4, 15-13
1949: Margaret Osborne duPont def. Doris Hart 6-4, 6-1
1950: Margaret Osborne duPont def. Doris Hart 6-3, 6-3
1951: Maureen Connolly def. Shirley Fry Irvin 6-3, 1-6, 6-4
1952: Maureen Connolly def. Doris Hart 6-3, 7-5
1953: Maureen Connolly def. Doris Hart 6-2, 6-4
1954: Doris Hart def. Louise Brough Clapp 6-8, 6-1, 8-6
1955: Doris Hart def. Patricia Ward Hales 6-1, 6-2

1956: Shirley Fry Irvin def. Althea Gibson 6-3, 6-4
1957: Althea Gibson def. Louise Brough Clapp 6-3, 6-2
1958: Althea Gibson def. Darlene Hard 3-6, 6-1, 6-2
1959: Maria Bueno def. Christine Truman 6-1, 6-4
1960: Darlene Hard def. Maria Bueno 6-4, 10-12, 6-4
1961: Darlene Hard def. Ann Haydon-Jones 6-3, 6-4
1962: Margaret Smith def. Darlene Hard 9-7, 6-4
1963: Maria Bueno def. Margaret Smith 7-5, 6-4
1964: Maria Bueno def. Carole Caldwell Graebner 6-1, 6-0
1965: Margaret Smith def. Billie Jean King 8-6, 7-5
1966: Maria Bueno def. Nancy Richey 6-3, 6-1
1967: Billie Jean King def. Ann Haydon-Jones 11-9, 6-4

Open Era

1968: Virginia Wade def. Billie Jean King 6-4, 6-2
1969: Margaret Smith Court def. Nancy Richey 6-2, 6-2
1970: Margaret Smith Court def. Rosie Casals 6-2, 2-6, 6-1
1971: Billie Jean King def. Rosie Casals 6-4, 7-6
1972: Billie Jean King def. Kerry Melville 6-3, 7-5
1973: Margaret Smith Court def. Evonne Goolagong 7-6, 5-7, 6-2
1974: Billie Jean King def. Evonne Goolagong 3-6, 6-3, 7-5
1975: Chris Evert def. Evonne Goolagong-Cawley 5-7, 6-4, 6-2
1976: Chris Evert def. Evonne Goolagong-Cawley 6-3, 6-0
1977: Chris Evert def. Wendy Turnbull 7-6, 6-2
1978: Chris Evert def. Pam Shriver 7-5, 6-4
1979: Tracy Austin def. Chris Evert-Lloyd 6-4, 6-3
1980: Chris Evert-Lloyd def. Hana Mandlikova 5-7, 6-1, 6-1
1981: Tracy Austin def. Martina Navratilova 1-6, 7-6^4, 7-6^1
1982: Chris Evert-Lloyd def. Hana Mandlikova 6-3, 6-1
1983: Martina Navratilova def. Chris Evert-Lloyd 6-1, 6-3
1984: Martina Navratilova def. Chris Evert-Lloyd 4-6, 6-4, 6-4
1985: Hana Mandlikova def. Martina Navratilova 7-6^3, 1-6, 7-6^2
1986: Martina Navratilova def. Helena Sukova 6-3, 6-2
1987: Martina Navratilova def. Steffi Graf 7-6^4, 6-1
1988: Steffi Graf def. Gabriela Sabatini 6-3, 3-6, 6-1
1989: Steffi Graf def. Martina Navratilova 3-6, 7-5, 6-1
1990: Gabriela Sabatini def. Steffi Graf 6-2, 7-6^4

1991: Monica Seles def. Martina Navratilova 7-6^1, 6-1
1992: Monica Seles def. Arantxa Sanchez Vicario 6-3, 6-3
1993: Steffi Graf def. Helena Sukova 6-3, 6-3
1994: Arantxa Sanchez Vicario def. Steffi Graf 1-6, 7-6^3, 6-4
1995: Steffi Graf def. Monica Seles 7-6^5, 0-6, 6-3
1996: Steffi Graf def. Monica Seles 7-5, 6-4
1997: Martina Hingis def. Venus Williams 6-0, 6-4
1998: Lindsay Davenport def. Martina Hingis 6-3, 7-5
1999: Serena Williams def. Martina Hingis 6-3, 7-6^4
2000: Venus Williams def. Lindsay Davenport 6-4, 7-5
2001: Venus Williams def. Serena Williams 6-2, 6-4
2002: Serena Williams def. Venus Williams 6-4, 6-3
2003: Justine Henin-Hardenne def. Kim Clijsters 7-5, 6-1
2004: Svetlana Kuznetsova def. Elena Dementieva 6-3, 7-5
2005: Kim Clijsters def. Mary Pierce 6-3, 6-1
2006: Maria Sharapova def. Justine Henin-Hardenne 6-4, 6-4
2007: Justine Henin def. Svetlana Kuznetsova 6-1, 6-3
2008: Serena Williams def. Jelena Jankovic 6-4, 7-5
2009: Kim Clijsters Lynch def. Caroline Wozniacki 7-5, 6-3
2010: Kim Clijsters Lynch def. Vera Zvonareva 6-2, 6-1
2011: Samantha Stosur def. Serena Williams 6-2, 6-3
2012: Serena Williams def. Victoria Azarenka 6-2, 2-6, 7-5
2013: Serena Williams def. Victoria Azarenka 7-5, 6-7^6, 6-1
2014: Serena Williams def. Caroline Wozniacki 6-3, 6-3
2015 : Flavia Pennetta def. Roberta Vinci 7-6^4, 6-2

The challenge round was played at the US Championships from 1888 until 1918; the defending champion was automatically qualified for the final (without playing any other match). All other players were engaged in the tournament and the finalist was then opposed to the previous year's champion. The current year's champion was the winner of that "second" final. When the defending champion forfeited, the tournament's new champion was the winner of the single elimination phase. This happened in 1893, 1899, 1900, 1905, 1906 and 1907.

All winners

1: Ellen Hansell (1887)
2: Bertha Townsend (1888, 1889)
3: Ellen Roosevelt (1890)
4: Mabel Cahill (1891, 1892)
5: Aline Terry (1893)
6: Helen Hellwig (1894)
7: Juliette Atkinson (1895, 1897, 1898)
8: Elisabeth Moore (1896, 1901, 1903, 1905)
9: Marion Jones (1899, 1902)
10: Myrtle McAteer (1900)
11: May Sutton Bundy (1904)
12: Helen Homans (1906)
13: Evelyn Sears (1907)
14: Maud Barger Wallach (1908)
15: Hazel Hotchkiss (then wed. Wightman) (1909, 1910, 1911, 1919)
16: Mary Kendall Browne (1912, 1913, 1914)
17: Mollie Bjurstedt Mallory (1915, 1916, 1917, 1918, 1920, 1921, 1922, 1926)
18: Helen Wills (then wed. Moody) (1923, 1924, 1925, 1927, 1928, 1929, 1931)
19: Betty Nuthall (1930)
20: Helen Hull Jacobs (1932, 1933, 1934, 1935)
21: Alice Marble (1936, 1938, 1939, 1940)
22: Anita Lizana (1937)
23: Sarah Palfrey Cooke (1941, 1945)
24: Pauline Betz Addie (1942, 1943, 1944, 1946)
25: Louise Brough Clapp (1947)
26: Margaret Osborne duPont (1948, 1949, 1950)
27: Maureen Connolly (1951, 1952, 1953)
28: Doris Hart (1954, 1955)
29: Shirley Fry Irvin (1956) (tournament's Senior to this day)
30: Althea Gibson (1957, 1958)
31: Maria Bueno (1959, 1963, 1964, 1966)
32: Darlene Hard (1960, 1961)
33: Margaret Smith (then wed. Court) (1962, 1965, 1969, 1970, 1973)
34: Billie Jean King (1967, 1971, 1972, 1974)
35: Virginia Wade (1968)
36: Chris Evert (then wed. Lloyd) (1975, 1976, 1977, 1978, 1980, 1982)

37: Tracy Austin (1979, 1981)
38: Martina Navratilova (1983, 1984, 1986, 1987)
39: Hana Mandlikova (1985)
40: Steffi Graf (1988, 1989, 1993, 1995, 1996)
41: Gabriela Sabatini (1990)
42: Monica Seles (1991, 1992)
43: Arantxa Sanchez Vicario (1994)
44: Martina Hingis (1997)
45: Lindsay Davenport (1998)
46: Serena Williams (1999, 2002, 2008, 2012, 2013, 2014)
47: Venus Williams (2000, 2001)
48: Justine Henin (2003, 2007)
49: Svetlana Kuznetsova (2004)
50: Kim Clijsters (2005, 2009, 2010)
51: Maria Sharapova (2006)
52: Samantha Stosur (2011)
53 : Flavia Pennetta (2015)

129 tournaments have been played.

Champions who were single at the time of their first victory have been listed under their maiden names. Their wedded names are quoted in brackets.

The tournament's senior is Shirley Fry Irvin, from the USA, 29th champion in 1956, born June 30, 1927 (88 years old).

US OPEN

Men's Singles

US Championships

1881: Richard Sears def. William Glyn 6-0, 6-3, 6-2
1882: Richard Sears def. Clarence Clark 6-1, 6-4, 6-0
1883: Richard Sears def. James Dwight 6-2, 6-0, 9-7
1884: Richard Sears def. Howard Taylor 6-0, 1-6, 6-0, 6-2
1885: Richard Sears def. Godfrey Brinley 6-3, 4-6, 6-0, 6-3
1886: Richard Sears def. Livingston Beeckman 4-6, 6-1, 6-3, 6-4
1887: Richard Sears def. Henry Slocum 6-1, 6-3, 6-2
1888: Henry Slocum def. Richard Sears, walkover
    1888: Henry Slocum def. Howard Taylor 6-4, 6-1, 6-0
1889: Henry Slocum def. Quincy Shaw 6-3, 6-1, 4-6, 6-2
1890: Oliver Campbell def. Henry Slocum 6-2, 4-6, 6-3, 6-1
1891: Oliver Campbell def. Clarence Hobart 2-6, 7-5, 7-9, 6-1, 6-2
1892: Oliver Campbell def. Fred Hovey 7-5, 3-6, 6-3, 7-5
1893: Robert Wrenn def. Oliver Campbell, walkover
    1893: Robert Wrenn def. Fred Hovey 6-4, 3-6, 6-4, 6-4
1894: Robert Wrenn def. Manliff Goodbody 6-8, 6-1, 6-4, 6-4
1895: Fred Hovey def. Robert Wrenn 6-3, 6-2, 6-4
1896: Robert Wrenn def. Fred Hovey 7-5, 3-6, 6-0, 1-6, 6-1
1897: Robert Wrenn def. Wilberforce Eaves 4-6, 8-6, 6-3, 2-6, 6-2
1898: Malcolm Whitman def. Robert Wrenn, walkover
    1898: Malcolm Whitman def. Dwight Davis 3-6, 6-2, 6-2, 6-1
1899: Malcolm Whitman def. Parmly Paret 6-1, 6-2, 3-6, 7-5
1900: Malcolm Whitman def. William Larned 6-4, 1-6, 6-2, 6-2
1901: William Larned def. Malcolm Whitman, walkover
    1901: William Larned def. Beals Wright 6-2, 6-8, 6-4, 6-4
1902: William Larned def. Reggie Doherty 4-6, 6-2, 6-4, 8-6
1903: Laurie Doherty def. William Larned 6-0, 6-3, 10-8
1904: Holcombe Ward def. Laurie Doherty, walkover
    1904: Holcombe Ward def. William Clothier 10-8, 6-4, 9-7
1905: Beals Wright def. Holcombe Ward 6-2, 6-1, 11-9
1906: William Clothier def. Beals Wright 6-3, 6-0, 6-4

1907: William Larned def. William Clothier, walkover
1907: William Larned def. Robert LeRoy 6-2, 6-2, 6-4
1908: William Larned def. Beals Wright 6-1, 6-2, 8-6
1909: William Larned def. William Clothier 6-1, 6-2, 5-7, 1-6, 6-1
1910: William Larned def. Tom Bundy 6-1, 5-7, 6-0, 6-8, 6-1
1911: William Larned def. Maurice McLoughlin 6-4, 6-4, 6-2
1912: Maurice McLoughlin def. Wallace Johnson 3-6, 2-6, 6-2, 6-4, 6-2
1913: Maurice McLoughlin def. Richard Norris Williams 6-4, 5-7, 6-3, 6-1
1914: Richard Norris Williams def. Maurice McLoughlin 6-3, 8-6, 10-8
1915: Bill Johnston def. Maurice McLoughlin 1-6, 6-0, 7-5, 10-8
1916: Richard Norris Williams def. Bill Johnston 4-6, 6-4, 0-6, 6-2, 6-4
1917: Robert Lindley Murray def. Nathaniel Niles 5-7, 8-6, 6-3, 6-3
1918: Robert Lindley Murray def. William Tilden 5-7, 8-6, 6-3, 6-3
1919: Bill Johnston def. William Tilden 6-4, 6-4, 6-3
1920: William Tilden def. Bill Johnston 6-1, 1-6, 7-5, 5-7, 6-3
1921: William Tilden def. Bill Johnston 6-1, 6-3, 6-1
1922: William Tilden def. Bill Johnston 4-6, 3-6, 6-2, 6-3, 6-4
1923: William Tilden def. Bill Johnston 6-4, 6-1, 6-4
1924: William Tilden def. Bill Johnston 6-1, 9-7, 6-2
1925: William Tilden def. Bill Johnston 4-6, 11-9, 6-3, 4-6, 6-3
1926: René Lacoste def. Jean Borotra 6-4, 6-0, 6-4
1927: René Lacoste def. William Tilden 11-9, 6-3, 11-9
1928: Henri Cochet def. Frank Hunter 4-6, 6-4, 3-6, 7-5, 6-3
1929: William Tilden def. Frank Hunter 3-6, 6-3, 4-6, 6-2, 6-4
1930: John Doeg def. Frank Shields 10-8, 1-6, 6-4, 16-14
1931: Ellsworth Vines def. George Lott 7-9, 6-3, 9-7, 7-5
1932: Ellsworth Vines def. Henri Cochet 6-4, 6-4, 6-4
1933: Fred Perry def. Jack Crawford 6-3, 11-13, 4-6, 6-0, 6-1
1934: Fred Perry def. Wilmer Allison 6-4, 6-3, 3-6, 1-6, 8-6
1935: Wilmer Allison def. Sidney Wood 6-2, 6-2, 6-3
1936: Fred Perry def. Donald Budge 2-6, 6-2, 8-6, 1-6, 10-8
1937: Donald Budge def. Gottfried von Cramm 6-1, 7-9, 6-1, 3-6, 6-1
1938: Donald Budge def. Gene Mako 6-3, 6-8, 6-2, 6-1
1939: Bobby Riggs def. Welby Van Horn 6-4, 6-2, 6-4
1940: William McNeill def. Bobby Riggs 4-6, 6-8, 6-3, 6-3, 7-5
1941: Bobby Riggs def. Frank Kovacs 5-7, 6-1, 6-3, 6-3
1942: Ted Schroeder def. Frank Parker 8-6, 7-5, 3-6, 4-6, 6-2
1943: Joseph Hunt def. Jack Kramer 6-3, 6-8, 10-8, 6-0

1944: Frank Parker def. Bill Talbert 6-4, 3-6, 6-3, 6-3
1945: Frank Parker def. Bill Talbert 14-12, 6-1, 6-2
1946: Jack Kramer def. Tom Brown 9-7, 6-3, 6-0
1947: Jack Kramer def. Frank Parker 4-6, 2-6, 6-1, 6-0, 6-3
1948: Pancho Gonzalez def. Erik Sturgess 6-2, 6-3, 14-12
1949: Pancho Gonzales def. Ted Schroeder 16-18, 2-6, 6-1, 6-2, 6-4
1950: Arthur Larsen def. Herbert Flam 6-3, 4-6, 5-7, 6-4, 6-3
1951: Frank Sedgman def. Vic Seixas 6-4, 6-1, 6-1
1952: Frank Sedgman def. Gardnar Mulloy 6-1, 6-2, 6-3
1953: Tony Trabert def. Vic Seixas 6-3, 6-2, 6-3
1954: Vic Seixas def. Rex Hartwig 3-6, 6-2, 6-4, 6-4
1955: Tony Trabert def. Ken Rosewall 9-7, 6-3, 6-3
1956: Ken Rosewall def. Lewis Hoad 4-6, 6-2, 6-3, 6-3
1957: Mal Anderson def. Ashley Cooper 10-8, 7-5, 6-4
1958: Ashley Cooper def. Mal Anderson 6-2, 3-6, 4-6, 10-8, 8-6
1959: Neale Fraser def. Alex Olmedo 6-3, 5-7, 6-2, 6-4
1960: Neale Fraser def. Rod Laver 6-4, 6-4, 9-7
1961: Roy Emerson def. Rod Laver 7-5, 6-3, 6-2
1962: Rod Laver def. Roy Emerson 6-2, 6-4, 5-7, 6-4
1963: Rafael Osuna def. Frank Froehling 7-5, 6-4, 6-2
1964: Roy Emerson def. Fred Stolle 6-4, 6-1, 6-4
1965: Manuel Santana def. Cliff Drysdale 6-2, 7-9, 7-5, 6-1
1966: Fred Stolle def. John Newcombe 4-6, 12-10, 6-3, 6-4
1967: John Newcombe def. Clark Graebner 6-4, 6-4, 8-6

Open Era

1968: Arthur Ashe def. Tom Okker 14-12, 5-7, 6-3, 3-6, 6-3
1969: Rod Laver def. Tony Roche 7-9, 6-1, 6-2, 6-2
1970: Ken Rosewall def. Tony Roche 2-6, 6-4, 7-6$^{5-2}$, 6-3
1971: Stan Smith def. Jan Kodes 3-6, 6-3, 6-2, 7-6$^{5-3}$
1972: Ilie Nastase def. Arthur Ashe 3-6, 6-3, 6-7$^{1-5}$, 6-4, 6-3
1973: John Newcombe def. Jan Kodes 6-4, 1-6, 4-6, 6-2, 6-3
1974: Jimmy Connors def. Ken Rosewall 6-1, 6-0, 6-1
1975: Manuel Orantes def. Jimmy Connors 6-4, 6-3, 6-3
1976: Jimmy Connors def. Björn Borg 6-4, 3-6, 7-6^9, 6-4
1977: Guillermo Vilas def. Jimmy Connors 2-6, 6-3, 7-6^4, 6-0
1978: Jimmy Connors def. Björn Borg 6-4, 6-2, 6-2

1979: John McEnroe def. Vitas Gerulaitis 7-5, 6-3, 6-3
1980: John McEnroe def. Björn Borg 7-6^4, 6-1, 6-7^5, 5-7, 6-4
1981: John McEnroe def. Björn Borg 4-6, 6-2, 6-4, 6-3
1982: Jimmy Connors def. Ivan Lendl 6-3, 6-2, 4-6, 6-4
1983: Jimmy Connors def. Ivan Lendl 6-3, 6-7^2, 7-5, 6-0
1984: John McEnroe def. Ivan Lendl 6-3, 6-4, 6-1
1985: Ivan Lendl def. John McEnroe 7-6^1, 6-3, 6-4
1986: Ivan Lendl def. Miloslav Mecir 6-4, 6-2, 6-0
1987: Ivan Lendl def. Mats Wilander 6-7^7, 6-0, 7-6^4, 6-4
1988: Mats Wilander def. Ivan Lendl 6-4, 4-6, 6-3, 5-7, 6-4
1989: Boris Becker def. Ivan Lendl 7-6^2, 1-6, 6-3, 7-6^4
1990: Pete Sampras def. Andre Agassi 6-4, 6-3, 6-2
1991: Stefan Edberg def. Jim Courier 6-2, 6-4, 6-0
1992: Stefan Edberg def. Pete Sampras 3-6, 6-4, 7-6^5, 6-2
1993: Pete Sampras def. Cédric Pioline 6-4, 6-4, 6-3
1994: Andre Agassi def. Michael Stich 6-1, 7-6^5, 7-5
1995: Pete Sampras def. Andre Agassi 6-4, 6-3, 4-6, 7-5
1996: Pete Sampras def. Michael Chang 6-1, 6-4, 7-6^3
1997: Patrick Rafter def. Greg Rusedski 6-3, 6-2, 4-6, 7-5
1998: Patrick Rafter def. Mark Philippoussis 6-3, 3-6, 6-2, 6-0
1999: Andre Agassi def. Todd Martin 6-4, 6-7^5, 6-7^2, 6-3, 6-2
2000: Marat Safin def. Pete Sampras 6-4, 6-3, 6-3
2001: Lleyton Hewitt def. Pete Sampras 7-6^4, 6-1, 6-1
2002: Pete Sampras def. Andre Agassi 6-3, 6-4, 5-7, 6-4
2003: Andy Roddick def. Juan Carlos Ferrero 6-3, 7-6^2, 6-3
2004: Roger Federer def. Lleyton Hewitt 6-0, 7-6^3, 6-0
2005: Roger Federer def. Andre Agassi 6-3, 2-6, 7-6^1, 6-1
2006: Roger Federer def. Andy Roddick 6-2, 4-6, 7-5, 6-1
2007: Roger Federer def. Novak Djokovic 7-6^4, 7-6^2, 6-4
2008: Roger Federer def. Andy Murray 6-2, 7-5, 6-2
2009: Juan Martin Del Potro def. Roger Federer 3-6, 7-6^5, 4-6, 7-6^4, 6-2
2010: Rafael Nadal def. Novak Djokovic 6-4, 5-7, 6-4, 6-2
2011: Novak Djokovic def. Rafael Nadal 6-2, 6-4, 6-7^3, 6-1
2012: Andy Murray def. Novak Djokovic 7-6^{10}, 7-5, 2-6, 3-6, 6-2
2013: Rafael Nadal def. Novak Djokovic 6-2, 3-6, 6-4, 6-1
2014: Marin Cilic def. Kei Nishikori 6-3, 6-3, 6-3
2015 : Novak Djokovic def. Roger Federer 6-4, 5-7, 6-4, 6-4

The challenge round was played at the US Championships from 1884 until 1911; the defending champion was automatically qualified for the final (without playing any other match). All other players were engaged in the tournament and the finalist was then opposed to the previous year's champion. The current year's champion was the winner of that "second final". When the defending champion forfeited, the tournament's new champion was the winner of the single elimination phase. This happened in 1888, 1893, 1898, 1901, 1904 and 1907.

All winners

1: Richard Sears (1881, 1882, 1883, 1884, 1885, 1886, 1887)
2: Henry Slocum (1888, 1889)
3: Oliver Campbell (1890, 1891, 1892)
4: Robert Wrenn (1893, 1894, 1896, 1897)
5: Fred Hovey (1895)
6: Malcolm Whitman (1898, 1899, 1900)
7: William Larned (1901, 1902, 1907, 1908, 1909, 1910, 1911)
8: Laurie Doherty (1903)
9: Holcombe Ward (1904)
10: Beals Wright (1905)
11: William Clothier (1906)
12: Maurice McLoughlin (1912, 1913)
13: Richard Norris Williams (1914, 1916) (Titanic survivor)
14: Bill Johnston (1915, 1919)
15: Robert Lindley Murray (1917, 1918)
16: William Tilden (1920, 1921, 1922, 1923, 1924, 1925, 1929)
17: René Lacoste (1926, 1927)
18: Henri Cochet (1928)
19: John Doeg (1930)
20: Ellsworth Vines (1931, 1932)
21: Fred Perry (1933, 1934, 1936)
22: Wilmer Allison (1935)
23: Donald Budge (1937, 1938)
24: Bobby Riggs (1939, 1941)
25: William McNeill (1940)
26: Ted Schroeder (1942)
27: Joseph Hunt (1943)
28: Frank Parker (1944, 1945)
29: Jack Kramer (1946, 1947)
30: Pancho Gonzalez (1948, 1949)
31: Arthur Larsen (1950)
32: Frank Sedgman (1951, 1952)
33: Tony Trabert (1953, 1955)
34: Vic Seixas (1954) (tournament's Senior to this day)
35: Ken Rosewall (1956, 1970)
36: Mal Anderson (1957)

37: Ashley Cooper (1958)
38: Neale Fraser (1959, 1960)
39: Roy Emerson (1961, 1964)
40: Rod Laver (1962, 1969)
41: Rafael Osuna (1963)
42: Manuel Santana (1965)
43: Fred Stolle (1966)
44: John Newcombe (1967, 1973)
45: Arthur Ashe (1968)
46: Stan Smith (1971)
47: Ilie Nastase (1972)
48: Jimmy Connors (1974, 1976, 1978, 1982, 1983)
49: Manuel Orantes (1975)
50: Guillermo Vilas (1977)
51: John McEnroe (1979, 1980, 1981, 1984)
52: Ivan Lendl (1985, 1986, 1987)
53: Mats Wilander (1988)
54: Boris Becker (1989)
55: Pete Sampras (1990, 1993, 1995, 1996, 2002)
56: Stefan Edberg (1991, 1992)
57: Andre Agassi (1994, 1999)
58: Patrick Rafter (1997, 1998)
59: Marat Safin (2000)
60: Lleyton Hewitt (2001)
61: Andy Roddick (2003)
62: Roger Federer (2004, 2005, 2006, 2007, 2008)
63: Juan Martin Del Potro (2009)
64: Rafael Nadal (2010, 2013)
65: Novak Djokovic (2011, 2015)
66: Andy Murray (2012)
67: Marin Cilic (2014)

135 tournaments have been played.

The tournament's senior is Vic Seixas, from the USA, 34th champion in 1954, born August 30, 1923 (92 years old).

TO SUM IT UP

Australian Open:

89 years of women's singles - 42 champions,
103 years of men's singles - 60 champions.

Roland-Garros:

108 years of women's singles - 54 champions,
114 years of men's singles - 60 champions.

Wimbledon:

122 years of women's singles - 45 champions,
129 years of men's singles - 65 champions.

US Open:

129 years of women's singles - 53 champions,
135 years of men's singles - 67 champions.

Grand total:
448 women's tournaments - 121 champions,
 481 men's tournaments - 160 champions.

(statistics to date, 2015 US Open included).

RESULT TALLY AND STATISTICS

The results of all grand slams have been entered in tables, and various statistics have been extracted in order to celebrate tennis over the years.

WOMEN'S RESULTS TALLY (in alphabetical order)

These figures show the number of times every champion was a winner in each tournament, and the total of all Grand Slam tournament wins for every champion.

At the bottom of the last table you can see the number of tournaments that have been played at every event to date.

A. O = Australian Open
R.G = Roland Garros
W = Wimbledon
US = US Open

LADIES CHAMPIONS	A.O	R.G	W	US	Total
Nelly ADAMSON LANDRY		1			1
Daphne AKHURST COZENS	5				5
Juliette ATKINSON				3	3
Cilly AUSSEM		1	1		2
Tracy AUSTIN				2	2
Victoria AZARENKA	2				2
Maud BARGER WALLACH				1	1
Sue BARKER		1			1
Marion BARTOLI			1		1
Pauline BETZ ADDIE			1	4	5
Blanche BINGLEY HILLYARD			6		6
Molla BJURSTEDT MALLORY				8	8
Shirley BLOOMER		1			1
Dora BOOTHBY			1		1
Kornelia BOUMAN		1			1
Esna BOYD ROBERTSON	1				1

LADIES CHAMPIONS	A.O	R.G	W	US	Total
Marguerite BROQUEDIS		2			2
Louise BROUGH CLAPP	1		4	1	6
Maria BUENO			3	4	7
Dorothy BUNDY CHENEY	1				1
Mabel CAHILL				2	2
Patricia CANNING TODD		1			1
Jennifer CAPRIATI	2	1			3
Mary CARTER REITANO	2				2
Kim CLIJSTERS	1			3	4
Maureen CONNOLLY	1	2	3	3	9
Charlotte COOPER STERRY			5		5
Thelma COYNE LONG	2				2
Lindsay DAVENPORT	1		1	1	3
Lottie DOD			5		5
Françoise DURR		1			1

LADIES CHAMPIONS	A.O	R.G	W	US	Total
Chris EVERT	2	7	3	6	**18**
Shirley FRY IRVIN	1	1	1	1	**4**
Althea GIBSON		1	2	2	**5**
Kate GILLOU FENWICK		4			**4**
P. GIROD		1			**1**
Evonne GOOLAGONG-CAWLEY	4	1	2		**7**
Steffi GRAF	4	6	7	5	**22**
Helen HANSELL				1	**1**
Karen HANTZE SUSMAN			1		**1**
Darlene HARD		1		2	**3**
Doris HART	1	2	1	2	**6**
Joan HARTIGAN BATHURST	3				**3**
Ann HAYDON-JONES		2	1		**3**
Helen HELLWIG				1	**1**
Justine HENIN	1	4		2	**7**

LADIES CHAMPIONS	A.O	R.G	W	US	Total
Martina HINGIS	3		1	1	5
Helen HOMANS				1	1
Emily HOOD WESTACOOT	1				1
Hazel HOTCHKISS WIGHTMAN				4	4
Helen HULL JACOBS			1	4	5
Ana IVANOVIC		1			1
Mima JAUSOVEC		1			1
Marion JONES FARQUHAR				2	2
Barbara JORDAN	1				1
Mary KENDALL BROWNE				3	3
Thérèse de KERMEL (Comtesse) (née Villard)		1			1
Billie Jean KING (née Moffitt)	1	1	6	4	12
Zsuzsa KORMOCZY		1			1
Hilde KRAHWINKEL SPERLING		3			3
Svetlana KUZNETSOVA		1		1	2

LADIES CHAMPIONS	A.O	R.G	W	US	Total
Petra KVITOVA			2		2
Dorothea LAMBERT CHAMBERS (née Douglass)			7		7
Sylvia LANCE HARPER	1				1
Suzanne LENGLEN		6	6		12
Na LI	1	1			2
Anita LIZANA				1	1
Iva MAJOLI		1			1
Hana MANDLIKOVA	2	1		1	4
Alice MARBLE			1	4	5
Conchita MARTINEZ			1		1
Adine MASSON		5			5
Simonne MATHIEU		2			2
Jeanne MATTHEY		4			4
Amélie MAURESMO	1		1		2
Myrtle McATEER				1	1

LADIES CHAMPIONS	A.O	R.G	W	US	Total
Coral McINNES BUTTSWORTH	2				2
Kathleen McKANE GODFREE			2		2
Kerry MELVILLE REID	1				1
Margaret MOLESWORTH	2				2
Elisabeth MOORE				4	4
Angela MORTIMER	1	1	1		3
Anastasia MYSKINA		1			1
Martina NAVRATILOVA	3	2	9	4	18
Jana NOVOTNA			1		1
Betty NUTHALL				1	1
Chris O'NEIL	1				1
Margaret OSBORNE duPONT		2	1	3	6
Sarah PALFREY COOKE				2	2
Flavia PENNETTA				1	1
Beryl PENROSE	1				1

LADIES CHAMPIONS	A.O	R.G	W	US	Total
Mary PIERCE	1	1			2
Hélène PREVOST		1			1
Lena RICE			1		1
Nancy RICHEY	1	1			2
Muriel ROBB			1		1
Ellen ROOSEVELT				1	1
Dorothy ROUND LITTLE	1		2		3
Virginia RUZICI		1			1
Gabriela SABATINI				1	1
Arantxa SANCHEZ VICARIO		3		1	4
Francesca SCHIAVONE		1			1
Margaret SCRIVEN		2			2
Evelyn SEARS				1	1
Monica SELES	4	3		2	9
Maria SHARAPOVA	1	2	1	1	5

LADIES CHAMPIONS	A.O	R.G	W	US	Total
Margaret SMITH COURT	11	5	3	5	24
Samantha STOSUR				1	1
May SUTTON BUNDY			2	1	3
Aline TERRY				1	1
Ethel THOMSON LARCOMBE			1		1
Bertha TOWNSEND				2	2
Christine TRUMAN		1			1
Lesley TURNER BOWREY		2			2
Julie VLASTO		1			1
Virginia WADE	1		1	1	3
Maud WATSON			2		2
Serena WILLIAMS	6	3	6	6	21
Venus WILLIAMS			5	2	7
Helen WILLS MOODY		4	8	7	19
Nancye WYNNE BOLTON	6				6
TOTAL	89	108	122	129	448

MEN'S RESULTS TALLY (in alphabetical order)

These figures show the number of times every champion was a winner in each tournament, and the total of all Grand Slam tournament wins for every champion.

At the bottom of the last table you can see the number of tournaments that have been played at every event to date.

A. O = Australian Open
R.G = Roland Garros
W = Wimbledon
US = US Open

MEN CHAMPIONS	A.O	R.G	W	US	Total
Andre AGASSI	4	1	1	2	8
Fred ALEXANDER	1				1
Wilmer ALLISON				1	1
James ANDERSON	3				3
Mal ANDERSON				1	1
Jozsef ASBOTH		1			1
Arthur ASHE	1		1	1	3
Paul AYME		4			4
Wilfred BADDELEY			3		3
Boris BECKER	2		3	1	6
Marcel BERNARD		1			1
François BLANCHY		1			1
Björn BORG		6	5		11
Jean BOROTRA	1	2	2		5
Bill BOWREY	1				1

MEN CHAMPIONS	A.O	R.G	W	US	Total
H. BRIGGS		1			1
John BROMWICH	2				2
Norman BROOKES (Sir)	1		2		3
Sergi BRUGUERA		2			2
Donald BUDGE	1	1	2	2	6
Oliver CAMPBELL				3	3
Pat CASH			1		1
Michael CHANG		1			1
Marin CILIC				1	1
William CLOTHIER				1	1
Henri COCHET		5	2	1	8
Jimmy CONNORS	1		2	5	8
Ashley COOPER	2		1	1	4
Albert COSTA		1			1
Jim COURIER	2	2			4

MEN CHAMPIONS	A.O	R.G	W	US	Total
Jack CRAWFORD	4	1	1		6
Sven DAVIDSON		1			1
Max DECUGIS		8			8
Juan Martin DEL POTRO				1	1
Novak DJOKOVIC	5		3	2	10
John DOEG				1	1
Laurie DOHERTY			5	1	6
Reggie DOHERTY			4		4
Jaroslav DROBNY		2	1		3
Stefan EDBERG	2		2	2	6
Mark EDMONDSON	1				1
Roy EMERSON	6	2	2	2	12
Bob FALKENBURG			1		1
Roger FEDERER	4	1	7	5	17
Juan Carlos FERRERO		1			1

MEN CHAMPIONS	A.O	R.G	W	US	Total
Neale FRASER			1	2	3
Gaston GAUDIO		1			1
Rhys GEMMEL	1				1
Maurice GERMOT		3			3
Vitas GERULAITIS	1				1
Andres GIMENO		1			1
André GOBERT		2			2
Andres GOMEZ		1			1
Pancho GONZALEZ				2	2
Arthur GORE			3		3
Spencer GORE			1		1
Colin GREGORY (Docteur)	1				1
Frank HADOW			1		1
Willoughby HAMILTON			1		1
John HARTLEY			2		2

MEN CHAMPIONS	A.O	R.G	W	US	Total
John HAWKES	1				1
Rodney HEATH	2				2
Henner HENKEL		1			1
Lleyton HEWITT			1	1	2
Lewis HOAD	1	1	2		4
Fred HOVEY				1	1
Joseph HUNT				1	1
Goran IVANISEVIC			1		1
Thomas JOHANSSON	1				1
Bill JOHNSTON			1	2	3
Yevgeny KAFELNIKOV	1	1			2
Algernon KINGSCOTE	1				1
Jan KODES		2	1		3
Petr KORDA	1				1
Richard KRAJICEK			1		1

MEN CHAMPIONS	A.O	R.G	W	US	Total
Jack KRAMER			1	2	3
Johan KRIEK	2				2
Gustavo KUERTEN		3			3
René LACOSTE		3	2	2	7
William LARNED				7	7
Arthur LARSEN				1	1
Rod LAVER	3	2	4	2	11
Herbert LAWFORD			1		1
Ivan LENDL	2	3		3	8
Gordon LOWE (Sir) (2ème Baronet)	1				1
Harold MAHONY			1		1
John McENROE			3	4	7
Vivian McGRATH	1				1
Ken McGREGOR	1				1
Chuck McKINLEY			1		1

MEN CHAMPIONS	A.O	R.G	W	US	Total
Maurice McLOUGHLIN				2	2
William McNEILL		1		1	2
Edgar MOON	1				1
Carlos MOYA		1			1
Andy MURRAY			1	1	2
Robert Lindley MURRAY				2	2
Thomas MUSTER		1			1
Rafael NADAL	1	9	2	2	14
Ilie NASTASE		1		1	2
John NEWCOMBE	2		3	2	7
Yannick NOAH		1			1
Arthur O'HARA WOOD	1				1
Pat O'HARA WOOD	2				2
Alex OLMEDO	1		1		2
Manuel ORANTES				1	1

MEN CHAMPIONS	A.O	R.G	W	US	Total
Rafael OSUNA				1	1
Dinny PAILS	1				1
Adriano PANATTA		1			1
James PARKE	1				1
Ernie PARKER	1				1
Frank PARKER		2		2	4
Gerald PATTERSON	1		2		3
Budge PATTY		1	1		2
Fred PERRY	1	1	3	3	8
Yvon PETRA			1		1
Nicola PIETRANGELI		2			2
Joshua PIM (Docteur)			2		2
Adrian QUIST	3				3
Patrick RAFTER				2	2
Ernest RENSHAW			1		1

MEN CHAMPIONS	A.O	R.G	W	US	Total
William RENSHAW			7		7
Laurent RIBOULET		1			1
Horace RICE	1				1
Bobby RIGGS			1	2	3
Tony ROCHE		1			1
Andy RODDICK				1	1
Mervyn ROSE	1	1			2
Ken ROSEWALL	4	2		2	8
Marat SAFIN	1			1	2
Jean SAMAZEUILH		1			1
Pete SAMPRAS	2		7	5	14
Manuel SANTANA		2	1	1	4
Dick SAVITT	1		1		2
Jean SCHOPFER		1			1
Ted SCHROEDER			1	1	2

MEN CHAMPIONS	A.O	R.G	W	US	Total
Richard SEARS				7	7
Frank SEDGMAN	2		1	2	5
Vic SEIXAS			1	1	2
Henry SLOCUM				2	2
Stan SMITH			1	1	2
Michael STICH			1		1
Fred STOLLE		1		1	2
Roscoe TANNER	1				1
Brian TEACHER	1				1
William TILDEN			3	7	10
Tony TRABERT		2	1	2	5
André VACHEROT		4			4
Michel VACHEROT		1			1
Guillermo VILAS	2	1		1	4
Ellsworth VINES			1	2	3

MEN CHAMPIONS	A.O	R.G	W	US	Total
Gottfried von CRAMM (Baron)		2			2
Holcombe WARD				1	1
Stanislas WAWRINKA	1	1			2
Malcolm WHITMAN				3	3
Mats WILANDER	3	3		1	7
Tony WILDING	2		4		6
Richard Norris WILLIAMS				2	2
Sidney WOOD			1		1
Robert WRENN				4	4
Beals WRIGHT				1	1
TOTAL	103	114	129	134	480

WOMEN'S GRAND SLAM

Three ladies champions have ever won a Grand Slam:
. Maureen Connolly in 1953,
. Margaret Smith Court in 1970,
. Steffi Graf in 1988.

In 1989, Steffi Graf was four points away from winning two Grand Slams in a row! This, as far as I know, was not spoken of much at the time.

This particular match was played in Paris on June 8th 1989:
Steffi Graf, who had won the Australian Open early in the year, was in the final at Roland-Garros, against Arantxa Sanchez Vicario.
In the third set, Steffi served for the match at 5-3, but lost her serve by love, and was unable to regain her lead.
She subsequently won Wimbledon and the US Open that year.

FOUR points in the 112 years (at the time) of Grand Slam history... It seems so petty...
Had those four points been won by Steffi Graf that day, it would have marked a prodigious event which wouldn't have faced challenge anytime soon.

"Career Grand Slam"

Only ten ladies champions have their names against each of the four major tournaments (for some of them, this was achieved over a number of years and is referred to as a "Career Grand Slam").

These ladies are listed below, in chronological order. The location and year of the last tournament won by each champion is in brackets.

1) Maureen Connolly (Roland-Garros 1953),
2) Doris Hart (US Championships 1954),
3) Shirley Fry Irvin (Australian Championships 1957),
4) Margaret Smith (then wed. Court) (Wimbledon 1963),
5) Billie Jean King (Roland-Garros 1972),
6) Chris Evert (Australian Open 1982),
7) Martina Navratilova (US Open 1983),
8) Steffi Graf (US Open 1988),

9) Serena Williams (Australian Open 2003),
10) Maria Sharapova (Roland-Garros 2012).

"Little Slam"

Eight women have achieved the "Little Slam" (in some cases, on several occasions), which involves winning 3 of the 4 majors in a calendar year:

. Helen Wills (then wed. Moody), 2 times:
- . in 1928 (missed Australian Championships)
- . in 1929 (missed Australian Championships).

. Margaret Smith (then wed. Court), 4 times:
- . in 1962 (missed Wimbledon)
- . in 1965 (missed Roland-Garros as a finalist)
- . in 1969 (missed Wimbledon)
- . in 1973 (missed Wimbledon).

. Billie Jean King:
- . in 1972 (missed Australian Open).

. Martina Navratilova, 2 times:
- . in 1983 (missed Roland-Garros)
- . in 1984 (missed Australian Open).

. Steffi Graf, 4 times:
- . in 1989 (missed Roland-Garros as a finalist and served for the match!)
- . in 1993 (missed Australian Open as a finalist)
- . in 1995 (missed Australian Open)
- . in 1996 (missed Australian Open).

. Monica Seles, 2 times:
- . in 1991 (missed Wimbledon)
- . in 1992 (missed Wimbledon as a finalist).

. Martina Hingis:
- . in 1997 (missed Roland-Garros as a finalist).

. Serena Williams, 2 times:
- . in 2002 (missed Australian Open)

. in 2015 (missed US Open).

List of achievements for the following champions:

. Steffi Graf has won every major tournament at least 4 times and has been credited with:
- . 1 Grand Slam
- . 3 Career Grand Slams
- . 4 Little Slams.

. Margaret Smith Court has won every major tournament at least 3 times and has been credited with:
- . 1 Grand Slam
- . 2 Career Grand Slams
- . 4 Little Slams.

. Maureen Connolly has won every major tournament at least once and has been credited with:
- . 1 Grand Slam.

. Serena Williams has won every major tournament at least 3 times and has been credited with:
- . 3 Career Grand Slams
- . 2 Little Slams.

. Martina Navratilova has won every major tournament at least 2 times and has been credited with:
- . 2 Career Grand Slams
- . 2 Little Slams.

. Chris Evert has won every major tournament at least 2 times and has been credited with:
- . 2 Career Grand Slams.

. Helen Wills Moody has been credited with:
- . 2 Little Slams.

. Monica Seles has been credited with:
- . 2 Little Slams.

MEN'S GRAND SLAM

Two men champions have ever won a Grand Slam:
. Donald Budge in 1938,
. Rod Laver, twice: in 1962 and 1969.

"Career Grand Slam"

Only seven men champions have their names against each of the four major tournaments (for some of them, this was achieved over a number of years and is referred to as a "Career Grand Slam").

These men are listed below, in chronological order. The location and year of the last tournament won by each champion is in brackets.

1) Fred Perry (Roland-Garros 1935),
2) Donald Budge (Roland-Garros 1938),
3) Rod Laver (US Championships 1962),
4) Roy Emerson (Wimbledon 1964),
5) Andre Agassi (Roland-Garros 1999),
6) Roger Federer (Roland-Garros 2009),
7) Rafael Nadal (US Open 2010).

Amazingly, no less than 35 YEARS had passed between Roy Emerson's (1964) and Andre Agassi's (1999) Career Grand Slams!
Previously, there had been a 24 YEAR gap between Donald Budge's (1938) and Rod Laver's (1962) Career Grand Slams.
For Budge and Laver, 1938 and 1962 are the respective years they won their real Grand Slam.

"Little Slam"

Eleven men have achieved the "little slam" (in some cases, on several occasions), which involves winning 3 of the 4 majors in a calendar year:

. Jack Crawford:
	. in 1933 (missed US Championships, as a finalist).

. Fred Perry:

. in 1934 (missed Roland-Garros).

. Tony Trabert:
    .. in 1955 (missed Australian Championships).

. Lewis Hoad:
    . in 1956 (missed US Championships, as a finalist).

. Ashley Cooper:
    . in 1958 (missed Roland-Garros).

. Roy Emerson:
    . in 1964 (missed Roland-Garros).

. Jimmy Connors:
    . in 1974 (missed Roland-Garros).

. Mats Wilander:
    . in 1988 (missed Wimbledon).

. Roger Federer, 3 times:
    . in 2004 (missed Roland-Garros)
    . in 2006 (missed Roland Garros, as a finalist)
    . in 2007 (missed Roland-Garros, as a finalist).

. Rafael Nadal:
    . in 2010 (missed Australian Open).

. Novak Djokovic, 2 times:
    . in 2011 (missed Roland-Garros)
    . in 2015 (missed Roland-Garros, as a finalist).

List of achievements for the following champions:

. Rod Laver has won every major tournament at least 2 times and has been credited with:
    . 2 Grand Slams.

. Donald Budge has won every major tournament at least once and has been credited with:
    . 1 Grand Slam.

. Roy Emerson has won every major tournament at least 2 times and has been credited with:

- 2 Career Grand Slams.

- Roger Federer has won every major tournament at least once and has been credited with:
    - 1 Career Grand Slam
    - 3 Little Slams

- Novak Djokovic has been credited with:
    - 2 Little Slams.

It has been 46 years since the last Men's Grand Slam in 1969 (Rod Laver's second Grand Slam).

It has been 27 years since the last Women's Grand Slam in 1988 (Steffi Graf's Grand Slam). Incidentally, Steffi Graf was born in 1969!

ALL THE 121 WOMEN CHAMPIONS IN CHRONOLOGICAL ORDER

The following 121 ladies became champions of the Grand Slam era in the following order. The location and the year of the first tournament won by each champion are in brackets.

1: Maud Watson (Wimbledon 1884)
2: Blanche Bingley (then wed. Hillyard) (Wimbledon 1886)
3: Lottie Dod (Wimbledon 1887)
4: Ellen Hansell (US Championships 1887)
5: Bertha Townsend (US Championships 1888)
6: Lena Rice (Wimbledon 1890)
7: Ellen Roosevelt (US Championships 1890)
8: Mabel Cahill (US Championships 1891)
9: Aline Terry (US Championships 1893)
10: Helen Hellwig (US Championships 1894)
11: Charlotte Cooper Sterry (Wimbledon 1895)
12: Juliette Atkinson (US Championships 1895)
13: Elisabeth Moore (US Championships 1896)
14: Adine Masson (French Championships 1897)
15: Marion Jones (US Championships 1899)
16: Hélène Prévost (French Championships 1900)
17: Myrtle McAteer (US Championships 1900)
18: P. Girod (French Championships 1901)
19: Muriel Robb (Wimbledon 1902)
20: Dorothea Douglass (then wed. Lambert-Chambers) (Wimbledon 1903)
21: Kate Gillou (then wed. Fenwick) (French Championships 1904)
22: May Sutton Bundy (US Championships 1904)
23: Helen Homans (US Championships 1906)
24: Countess Thérèse de Kermel (French Championships 1907)
25: Evelyn Sears (US Championships 1907)
26: Maud Barger Wallach (US Championships 1908)
27: Jeanne Matthey (French Championships 1909)
28: Dora Boothby (Wimbledon 1909)
29: Hazel Hotchkiss (then wed. Wightman) (US Championships 1909)
30: Ethel Thomson Larcombe (Wimbledon 1912)

31: Mary Kendall Browne (US Championships 1912)
32: Marguerite Broquedis (French Championships 1913)
33: Molla Bjurstedt Mallory (US Championships 1915)
34: Suzanne Lenglen (Wimbledon 1919)
35: Margaret Molesworth (Australasian Championships 1922)
36: Helen Wills (then wed. Moody) (US Championships 1923)
37: Sylvia Lance Harper (Australasian Championships 1924)
38: Julie Vlasto (French Championships 1924)
39: Kathleen McKane Godfree (Wimbledon 1924)
40: Daphne Akhurst Cozens (Australasian Championships 1925)
41: Esna Boyd Robertson (Australian Championships 1927)
42: Kornelia Bouman (International French Championships 1927)
43: Betty Nuthall (US Championships 1930)
44: Coral McInnes Buttsworth (Australian Championships 1931)
45: Cilly Aussem (Roland-Garros 1931)
46: Helen Hull Jacobs (US Championships 1932)
47: Joan Hartigan Bathurst (Australian Championships 1933)
48: Margaret Scriven (Roland-Garros 1933)
49: Dorothy Round Little (Wimbledon 1934)
50: Hilde Krahwinkel Sperling (Roland-Garros 1935)
51: Alice Marble (US Championships 1936)
52: Nancye Wynne Bolton (Australian Championships 1937)
53: Anita Lizana (US Championships 1937)
54: Dorothy Bundy (Australian Championships 1938)
55: Simonne Mathieu (Roland-Garros 1938)
56: Emily Hood Westacoot (Australian Championships 1939)
57: Sarah Palfrey Cooke (US Championships 1941)
58: Pauline Betz Addie (US Championships 1942)
59: Margaret Osborne (then wed. duPont) (Roland-Garros 1946)
60: Patricia Canning Todd (Roland-Garros 1947)
61: Louise Brough Clapp (US Championships 1947)
62: Nelly Adamson Landry (Roland-Garros 1948)
63: Doris Hart (Australian Championships 1949)
64: Shirley Fry Irvin (Roland-Garros 1951)
65: Maureen Connolly (US Championships 1951)
66: Thelma Coyne Long (Australian Championships 1952)
67: Beryl Penrose (Australian Championships 1955)
68: Angela Mortimer (Roland-Garros 1955)

69: Mary Carter Reitano (Australian Championships 1956)
70: Althea Gibson (Roland-Garros 1956)
71: Shirley Bloomer (Roland-Garros 1957)
72: Zsuzsa Kormoczy (Roland-Garros 1958)
73: Christine Truman (Roland-Garros 1959)
74: Maria Bueno (Wimbledon 1959)
75: Margaret Smith (then wed. Court) (Australian Championships 1960)
76: Darlene Hard (Roland-Garros 1960)
77: Ann Haydon-Jones (Roland-Garros 1961)
78: Karen Hantze Susman (Wimbledon 1962)
79: Lesley Turner (Roland-Garros 1963)
80: Billie Jean King (Wimbledon 1966)
81: Nancy Richey (Australian Championships 1967)
82: Françoise Durr (Roland-Garros 1967)
83: Virginia Wade (US Open 1968)
84: Evonne Goolagong (then wed. Cawley) (Wimbledon 1971)
85: Chris Evert (then wed. Lloyd) (Roland-Garros 1974)
86: Sue Barker (Roland-Garros 1976)
87: Kerry Melville Reid (Australian Open 1977 January)
88: Mima Jausovec (Roland-Garros 1977)
89: Virginia Ruzici (Roland-Garros 1978)
90: Martina Navratilova (Wimbledon 1978)
91: Chris O'Neil (Australian Open 1978 December)
92: Tracy Austin (US Open 1979)
93: Barbara Jordan (Australian Open 1979 December)
94: Hana Mandlikova (Australian Open 1980 December)
95: Steffi Graf (Roland-Garros 1987)
96: Arantxa Sanchez Vicario (Roland-Garros 1989)
97: Monica Seles (Roland-Garros 1990)
98: Gabriela Sabatini (US Open 1990)
99: Conchita Martinez (Wimbledon 1994)
100: Mary Pierce (Australian Open 1995)
101: Martina Hingis (Australian Open 1997)
102: Iva Majoli (Roland-Garros 1997)
103: Jana Novotna (Wimbledon 1998)
104: Lindsay Davenport (US Open 1998)
105: Serena Williams (US Open 1999)
106: Venus Williams (Wimbledon 2000)

107: Jennifer Capriati (Australian Open 2001)
108: Justine Henin (Roland-Garros 2003)
109: Anastasia Myskina (Roland-Garros 2004)
110: Maria Sharapova (Wimbledon 2004)
111: Svetlana Kuznetsova (US Open 2004)
112: Kim Clijsters (US Open 2005)
113: Amélie Mauresmo (Australian Open 2006)
114: Ana Ivanovic (Roland-Garros 2008)
115: Francesca Schiavone (Roland-Garros 2010)
116: Li Na (Roland-Garros 2011)
117: Petra Kvitova (Wimbledon 2011)
118: Samantha Stosur (US Open 2011)
119: Victoria Azarenka (Australian Open 2012)
120: Marion Bartoli (Wimbledon 2013)
121 : Flavia Pennetta (US Open 2015).

(Statistics to date, 2015 US Open included).

Note the amazingly large amount of time between Champions 94 (Hana Mandlikova) and 95 (Steffi Graf).

Hana Mandlikova was first crowned during the December 1980 Australian Open.

Steffi Graf was first crowned during the 1987 Roland-Garros tournament.

Within this time frame, no less than TWENTY FOUR Grand Slam Tournaments were played and NOT ONE new champion was crowned!

These 24 tournaments were won by only four existing champions: Chris Evert won 7 of the titles, Martina Navratilova won 13, Tracy Austin won 1 and Hana Mandlikova won 3.

Within six years, 20 out of 24 titles were split between Evert and Navratilova!

This highlights the stronghold the two players had on Women's Tennis at the time.

This double supremacy is absolutely unique, given men's Tennis has not seen anything like it.

ALL THE 160 MEN CHAMPIONS IN CHRONOLOGICAL ORDER

The following 160 men became champions of the Grand Slam era in that particular order. The location and the year of the first tournament won by each champion are in brackets:

1: Spencer Gore (Wimbledon 1877)
2: Frank Hadow (Wimbledon 1878)
3: John Hartley (Wimbledon 1879)
4: William Renshaw (Wimbledon 1881)
5: Richard Sears (US Championships 1881)
6: Herbert Lawford (Wimbledon 1887)
7: Ernest Renshaw (Wimbledon 1888)
8: Henry Slocum (US Championships 1888)
9: Willoughby Hamilton (Wimbledon 1890)
10: Oliver Campbell (US Championships 1890)
11: H. Briggs (French Championships 1891)
12: Wilfred Baddeley (Wimbledon 1891)
13: Jean Schopfer (French Championships 1892)
14: Laurent Riboulet (French Championships 1893)
15: Joshua Pim (Wimbledon 1893)
16: Robert Wrenn (US Championships 1893)
17: André Vacherot (French Championships 1894)
18: Fred Hovey (US Championships 1895)
19: Harold Mahony (Wimbledon 1896)
20: Paul Aymé (French Championships 1897)
21: Reggie Doherty (Wimbledon 1897)
22: Malcolm Whitman (US Championships 1898)
23: Arthur Gore (Wimbledon 1901)
24: William Larned (US Championships 1901)
25: Michel Vacherot (French Championships 1902)
26: Laurie Doherty (Wimbledon 1902)
27: Max Decugis (French Championships 1903)
28: Holcombe Ward (US Championships 1904)
29: Maurice Germot (French Championships 1905)
30: Beals Wright (US Championships 1905)

31: Rodney Heath (Australasian Championships 1905 November)
32: William Clothier (US Championships 1906)
33: Tony Wilding (Australasian Championships 1906 December)
34: Norman Brookes (Wimbledon 1907)
35: Horace Rice (Australasian Championships 1907 August)
36: Fred Alexander (Australasian Championships 1908)
37: André Gobert (French Championships 1911)
38: James Parke (Australasian Championships 1912 January)
39: Maurice McLoughlin (US Championships 1912)
40: Ernie Parker (Australasian Championships 1913)
41: Richard Norris Williams (US Championships 1914) (Titanic's survivor)
42: Arthur O'Hara Wood (Australasian Championships 1914 November)
43: Bill Johnston (US Championships 1915)
44: Gordon Lowe (Australasian Championships 1915 August)
45: Robert Lindley Murray (US Championships 1917)
46: Gerald Patterson (Wimbledon 1919)
47: Algernon Kingscote (Australasian Championships 1919, played in January 1920)
48: Pat O'Hara Wood (Australasian Championships 1920 March)
49: William Tilden (Wimbledon 1920)
50: Jean Samazeuilh (French Championships 1921)
51: Rhys Gemmell (Australasian Championships 1921 December)
52: Henri Cochet (French Championships 1922)
53: James Anderson (Australasian Championships 1922 December)
54: François Blanchy (French Championships 1923)
55: Jean Borotra (French Championships 1924)
56: René Lacoste (International French Championships 1925)
57: John Hawkes (Australasian Championships 1926)
58: Colin Gregory (Australian Championships 1929)
59: Edgar Moon (Australian Championships 1930)
60: John Doeg (US Championships 1930)
61: Jack Crawford (Australian Championships 1931)
62: Sidney Wood (Wimbledon 1931)
63: Ellsworth Vines (US Championships 1931)
64: Fred Perry (US Championships 1933)
65: Gottfried von Cramm (Roland-Garros 1934)
66: Wilmer Allison (US Championships 1935)
67: Adrian Quist (Australian Championships 1936)
68: Vivian McGrath (Australian Championships 1937)

69: Henner Henkel (Roland-Garros 1937)
70: Donald Budge (Wimbledon 1937)
71: John Bromwich (Australian Championships 1939)
72: William McNeill (Roland-Garros 1939)
73: Bobby Riggs (Wimbledon 1939)
74: Ted Schroeder (US Championships 1942)
75: Joseph Hunt (US Championships 1943)
76: Frank Parker (US Championships 1944)
77: Yvon Petra (Wimbledon 1946)*
78: Marcel Bernard (Roland-Garros 1946)*
79: Jack Kramer (US Championships 1946)
80: Dinny Pails (Australian Championships 1947)
81: Jozsef Asboth (Roland-Garros 1947)
82: Bob Falkenburg (Wimbledon 1948)
83: Pancho Gonzalez (US Championships 1948)
84: Frank Sedgman (Australian Championships 1949)
85: Budge Patty (Roland-Garros 1950)
86: Arthur Larsen (US Championships 1950)
87: Dick Savitt (Australian Championships 1951)
88: Jaroslav Drobny (Roland-Garros 1951)
89: Ken McGregor (Australian Championships 1952)
90: Ken Rosewall (Australian Championships 1953)
91: Vic Seixas (Wimbledon 1953)
92: Tony Trabert (US Championships 1953)
93: Mervyn Rose (Australian Championships 1954)
94: Lewis Hoad (Australian Championships 1956)
95: Ashley Cooper (Australian Championships 1957)
96: Sven Davidson (Roland-Garros 1957)
97: Mal Anderson (US Championships 1957)
98: Alex Olmedo (Australian Championships 1959)
99: Nicola Pietrangeli (Roland-Garros 1959)
100: Neale Fraser (US Championships 1959)
101: Rod Laver (Australian Championships 1960)
102: Roy Emerson (Australian Championships 1961)
103: Manuel Santana (Roland-Garros 1961)
104: Chuck McKinley (Wimbledon 1963)
105: Rafael Osuna (US Championships 1963)
106: Fred Stolle (Roland-Garros 1965)

107: Tony Roche (Roland-Garros 1966)
108: John Newcombe (Wimbledon 1967)
109: Bill Bowrey (Australian Championships 1968)
110: Arthur Ashe (US Open 1968)
111: Jan Kodes (Roland-Garros 1970)
112: Stan Smith (US Open 1971)
113: Andres Gimeno (Roland-Garros 1972)
114: Ilie Nastase (US Open 1972)
115: Jimmy Connors (Australian Open 1974)
116: Björn Borg (Roland-Garros 1974)
117: Manuel Orantes (US Open 1975)
118: Mark Edmondson (Australian Open 1976)
119: Adriano Panatta (Roland-Garros 1976)
120: Roscoe Tanner (Australian Open 1977 January)
121: Guillermo Vilas (Roland-Garros 1977)
122: Vitas Gerulaitis (Australian Open 1977 December)
123: John McEnroe (US Open 1979)
124: Brian Teacher (Australian Open 1980 December)
125: Johan Kriek (Australian Open 1981 December)
126: Mats Wilander (Roland-Garros 1982)
127: Yannick Noah (Roland-Garros 1983)
128: Ivan Lendl (Roland-Garros 1984)
129: Boris Becker (Wimbledon 1985)
130: Stefan Edberg (Australian Open 1985 December)
131: Pat Cash (Wimbledon 1987)
132: Michael Chang (Roland-Garros 1989)
133: Andres Gomez (Roland-Garros 1990)
134: Pete Sampras (US Open 1990)
135: Jim Courier (Roland-Garros 1991)
136: Michael Stich (Wimbledon 1991)
137: Andre Agassi (Wimbledon 1992)
138: Sergi Bruguera (Roland-Garros 1993)
139: Thomas Muster (Roland-Garros 1995)
140: Yevgeny Kafelnikov (Roland-Garros 1996)
141: Richard Krajicek (Wimbledon 1996)
142: Gustavo Kuerten (Roland-Garros 1997)
143: Patrick Rafter (US Open 1997)
144: Petr Korda (Australian Open 1998)

145: Carlos Moya (Roland-Garros 1998)
146: Marat Safin (US Open 2000)
147: Goran Ivanisevic (Wimbledon 2001)
148: Lleyton Hewitt (US Open 2001)
149: Thomas Johansson (Australian Open 2002)
150: Albert Costa (Roland-Garros 2002)
151: Juan Carlos Ferrero (Roland-Garros 2003)
152: Roger Federer (Wimbledon 2003)
153: Andy Roddick (US Open 2003)
154: Gaston Gaudio (Roland-Garros 2004)
155: Rafael Nadal (Roland-Garros 2005)
156: Novak Djokovic (Australian Open 2008)
157: Juan Martin Del Potro (US Open 2009)
158: Andy Murray (US Open 2012)
159: Stanislas Wawrinka (Australian Open 2014)
160: Marin Cilic (US Open 2014).

*in 1946 and 1947, Wimbledon took place before Roland-Garros.

(Statistics to date, 2015 US Open included).

THE 4 GIANTS OF MODERN TENNIS

During the 70's and 80's, Chris Evert and Martina Navratilova dominated the world of women's Tennis.

By comparison, FOUR men have had a stronghold over men's Tennis between 2004 and 2013, and will more than likely remain at the forefront of tennis for a while yet. They are: Roger Federer, Rafael Nadal, Novak Djokovic and Andy Murray.

Between Wimbledon 2004 and the US Open 2013, 38 Grand Slam tournaments were played. 36 of these have been split between them!

The remaining two tournaments were won by Marat Safin (Australian Open 2005) and Juan Martin del Potro (US Open 2009).

It is worth noting: to date, 27 Grand Slam finals were played between two of those four dominating players... and there are probably more to come.

Out of those 27 finals, Nadal won 10 and lost 5, Djokovic won 9 and lost 7, Federer won 6 and lost 9, Murray won 2 and lost 6.

THE SENIORS

Australian Open:

Shirley Fry Irvin, 17th champion in 1957, born June 30, 1927, 88 years old.
Dick Savitt, 27th champion in 1951, born March 4, 1927, 88 years old.

Roland-Garros:

Shirley Fry Irvin, 20th champion in 1951, born June 30, 1927, 88 years old.
Budge Patty, 24th champion in 1950, born February 11, 1924, 91 years old.

Wimbledon:

Shirley Fry Irvin, 23rd champion in 1956, born June 30, 1927, 88 years old.
Vic Seixas, 35th champion in 1953, born August 30th, 1923, 92 years old.

US Open:

Shirley Fry Irvin, 29th champion in 1956, born June 30th, 1927, 88 years old.
Vic Seixas, 34th champion in 1954, born August 30th, 1923, 92 years old.

The youngest winners of a major, still playing

Petra Kvitova, born March 8, 1990, 25 years old,
Marin Cilic, born September 28, 1988, 27 years old.

REPRESENTED COUNTRIES

Women and men champions are now listed by their country of origin.

Some champions have won titles while still under their birth citizenships and have moved on into their careers under different citizenships.

Some champions are listed twice if required, depending on their citizenship at the time of a specific win.

Some countries have changed names and are listed under their current names.

Women Champions

1) USA: 42 champions (199 titles)

Juliette ATKINSON
Tracy AUSTIN
Maud BARGER WALLACH
Pauline BETZ ADDIE
Molla BJURSTEDT MALLORY* (US citizen for 6 out of her 8 Grand Slam titles)
Louise BROUGH CLAPP
Dorothy BUNDY CHENEY
Patricia CANNING TODD
Jennifer CAPRIATI
Maureen CONNOLLY
Lindsay DAVENPORT
Chris EVERT
Shirley FRY IRVIN
Althea GIBSON
Ellen HANSELL
Karen HANTZE SUSMAN
Darlene HARD
Doris HART
Helen HELLWIG
Helen HOMANS
Hazel HOTCHKISS WIGHTMAN
Helen HULL JACOBS
Marion JONES FARQUHAR
Barbara JORDAN

Mary KENDALL BROWNE
Billie Jean KING
Alice MARBLE
Myrtle McATEER
Elisabeth MOORE
Martina NAVRATILOVA* (US citizen for 16 out of her 18 Grand Slam titles)
Margaret OSBORNE duPONT
Sarah PALFREY COOKE
Nancy RICHEY
Ellen ROOSEVELT
Evelyn SEARS
Monica SELES* (US citizen for her ninth and last Grand Slam title)
May SUTTON BUNDY
Aline TERRY
Bertha TOWNSEND
Serena WILLIAMS
Venus WILLIAMS
Helen WILLS MOODY

2) United Kingdom: 18 champions (48 titles)

Sue BARKER
Blanche BINGLEY HILLYARD
Shirley BLOOMER
Dora BOOTHBY
Charlotte COOPER STERRY
Lottie DOD
Ann HAYDON-JONES
Dorothea LAMBERT-CHAMBERS
Kathleen McKANE GODFREE
Angela MORTIMER
Betty NUTHALL
Muriel ROBB
Dorothy ROUND LITTLE
Margaret SCRIVEN
Ethel THOMSON LARCOMBE
Christine TRUMAN
Virginia WADE

Maud WATSON

3) Australia: 17 champions (62 titles)

Daphne AKHURST COZENS
Esna BOYD ROBERTSON
Mary CARTER REITANO
Thelma COYNE LONG
Evonne GOOLAGONG-CAWLEY
Joan HARTIGAN BATHURST
Emily HOOD WESTACOOT
Sylvia LANCE HARPER
Coral McINNES BUTTSWORTH
Kerry MELVILLE REID
Margaret MOLESWORTH
Chris O'NEIL
Beryl PENROSE
Margaret SMITH COURT
Samantha STOSUR
Lesley TURNER BOWREY
Nancye WYNNE BOLTON

4) France: 15 champions (40 titles)

Nelly ADAMSON LANDRY (Belgian from birth, then French citizen by marriage before winning her unique Grand Slam title)
Marion BARTOLI
Marguerite BROQUEDIS
Françoise DURR
Kate GILLOU FENWICK
P. GIROD
Thérèse de KERMEL
Suzanne LENGLEN
Adine MASSON
Simonne MATHIEU
Jeanne MATTHEY
Amélie MAURESMO
Mary PIERCE
Hélène PREVOST

Julie VLASTO

5) Czech Republic: 4 champions (9 titles)

Petra KVITOVA
Hana MANDLIKOVA (after her retirement she became an Australian citizen by marriage)
Martina NAVRATILOVA* (Czech citizen for her 2 first titles; for the other 16, she was a US citizen)
Jana NOVOTNA

6) Germany: 3 champions (27 titles)

Cilly AUSSEM
Steffi GRAF
Hilde KRAHWINKEL SPERLING (German citizen from birth, then Danish citizen by marriage in December 1933, before winning her Grand Slam titles ; but she was quoted as a German citizen in the result tally)

6) Russia: 3 champions (8 titles)

Svetlana KUZNETSOVA
Anastasia MYSKINA
Maria SHARAPOVA

8) Belgium: 2 champions (11 titles)

Kim CLIJSTERS
Justine HENIN

8) Ireland: 2 champions (3 titles)

Mabel CAHILL
Lena RICE

8) Italy: 2 champions (2 titles)

Flavia PENNETTA
Francesca SCHIAVONE

8) Serbia: 2 champions (9 titles)

Ana IVANOVIC

Monica SELES* (Yugoslavian (Serbian) citizen, she won her 8 first Grand Slam titles as a Yugoslavian, before winning her ninth and last title as a US citizen)

8) Spain: 2 champions (5 titles)

Conchita MARTINEZ
Arantxa SANCHEZ VICARIO

13) Argentina: 1 champion (1 title)

Gabriela SABATINI

13) Belarus: 1 champion (2 titles)

Victoria AZARENKA

13) Brazil: 1 champion (7 titles)

Maria BUENO

13) Chile: 1 champion (1 title)

Anita LIZANA

13) China: 1 champion (2 titles)

LI Na

13) Croatia: 1 champion (1 title)

Iva MAJOLI

13) Hungary: 1 champion (1 title)

Zsuzsa KORMOCZY

13) Netherlands: 1 champion (1 title)

Kornelia BOUMAN

13) Norway: 1 champion (2 titles)

Molla BJURSTEDT MALLORY* (Norwegian citizen from birth, she won her 2 first Grand Slam titles as a Norwegian; for the other 6, she was a US citizen)

13) Romania: 1 champion (1 title)

Virginia RUZICI

13) Slovenia: 1 champion (1 title)

Mima JAUSOVEC

13) Switzerland: 1 champion (5 titles)

Martina HINGIS

24 DIFFERENT COUNTRIES

* Molla BJURSTEDT MALLORY, Martina NAVRATILOVA and Monica SELES are the only champions who have been quoted twice in this section, for having won tournaments under two different citizenships.

Men champions

1) USA: 49 champions (147 titles)

Andre AGASSI
Fred ALEXANDER
Wilmer ALLISON
Arthur ASHE
Donald BUDGE
Oliver CAMPBELL
Michael CHANG
William CLOTHIER
Jimmy CONNORS
Jim COURIER
John DOEG
Bob FALKENBURG
Vitas GERULAITIS
Pancho GONZALEZ
Fred HOVEY
Joseph HUNT
Bill JOHNSTON
Jack KRAMER
Johan KRIEK* (born South African, he was a US citizen for his second Grand Slam title)
William LARNED
Arthur LARSEN
John McENROE
Chuck McKINLEY
Maurice McLOUGHLIN
William McNEILL
Robert Lindley MURRAY
Alex OLMEDO (born Peruvian citizen, he won his 2 Grand Slam titles as a US citizen)
Frank PARKER
Budge PATTY
Bobby RIGGS
Andy RODDICK
Pete SAMPRAS
Dick SAVITT
Ted SCHROEDER

Richard SEARS
Vic SEIXAS
Henry SLOCUM
Stan SMITH
Roscoe TANNER
Brian TEACHER
William TILDEN
Tony TRABERT
Ellsworth VINES
Holcombe WARD
Malcolm WHITMAN
Richard Norris WILLIAMS
Sidney WOOD
Robert WRENN
Beals WRIGHT

2) Australia: 34 champions (100 titles)

James ANDERSON
Mal ANDERSON
Bill BOWREY
John BROMWICH
Norman BROOKES
Pat CASH
Ashley COOPER
Jack CRAWFORD
Mark EDMONDSON
Roy EMERSON
Neale FRASER
Rhys GEMMELL
John HAWKES
Rodney HEATH
Lleyton HEWITT
Lewis HOAD
Rod LAVER
Vivian McGRATH
Ken McGREGOR
Edgar MOON

John NEWCOMBE
Arthur O'HARA WOOD
Pat O'HARA WOOD
Dinny PAILS
Ernie PARKER
Gerald PATTERSON
Adrian QUIST
Patrick RAFTER
Horace RICE
Tony ROCHE
Mervyn ROSE
Ken ROSEWALL
Frank SEDGMAN
Fred STOLLE

3) France: 16 champions (49 titles)

Paul AYME
Marcel BERNARD
François BLANCHY
Jean BOROTRA
Henri COCHET
Max DECUGIS
Maurice GERMOT
André GOBERT
René LACOSTE
Yannick NOAH
Yvon PETRA
Laurent RIBOULET
Jean SAMAZEUILH
Jean SCHOPFER
André VACHEROT
Michel VACHEROT

3) United Kingdom: 16 champions (43 titles)

Wilfred BADDELEY
H. BRIGGS
Laurie DOHERTY

Reggie DOHERTY
Arthur GORE
Spencer GORE
Colin GREGORY
Frank HADOW
John HARTLEY
Algernon KINGSCOTE
Herbert LAWFORD
Gordon LOWE
Andy MURRAY
Fred PERRY
Ernest RENSHAW
William RENSHAW

5) Spain: 8 champions (25 titles)

Sergi BRUGUERA
Albert COSTA
Juan Carlos FERRERO
Andres GIMENO
Carlos MOYA
Rafael NADAL
Manuel ORANTES
Manuel SANTANA

6) Sweden: 5 champions (26 titles)

Björn BORG
Sven DAVIDSON
Stefan EDBERG
Thomas JOHANSSON
Mats WILANDER

7) Germany: 4 champions (10 titles)

Boris BECKER
Henner HENKEL
Michael STICH
Gottfried von CRAMM

7) Ireland: 4 champions (5 titles)

Willoughby HAMILTON
Harold MAHONY
James PARKE
Joshua PIM

9) Argentina: 3 champions (6 titles)

Juan Martin DEL POTRO
Gaston GAUDIO
Guillermo VILAS

9) Czech republic: 3 champions (12 titles)

Jan KODES
Petr KORDA
Ivan LENDL (Czech citizen for all his 8 Grand Slam titles; then he became a US citizen in July 1992)

11) Croatia: 2 champions (2 titles)

Marin CILIC
Goran IVANISEVIC

11) Italy: 2 champions (3 titles)

Adriano PANATTA
Nicola PIETRANGELI

11) Russia: 2 champions (4 titles)

Yevgeny KAFELNIKOV
Marat SAFIN

11) Switzerland: 2 champions (19 titles)

Roger FEDERER
Stanislas WAWRINKA

15) Austria: 1 champion (1 title)

Thomas MUSTER

15) Brazil: 1 champion (3 titles)

Gustavo KUERTEN

15) Ecuador: 1 champion (1 title)

Andres GOMEZ

15) Egypt: 1 champion (3 titles)

Jaroslav DROBNY (born Czech, then under "Protectorate of Bohemia and Moravia" (during WWII). He later became an Egyptian citizen and played as such from 1950 until 1959, winning his Grand Slam titles during this time. He then became a British citizen at the end of his career.

15) Hungary: 1 champion (1 title)

Jozsef ASBOTH

15) Mexico: 1 champion (1 title)

Rafael OSUNA

15) Netherlands: 1 champion (1 title)

Richard KRAJICEK

15) New Zealand: 1 champion (6 titles)

Tony WILDING

15) Romania: 1 champion (2 titles)

Ilie NASTASE

15) Serbia: 1 champion (10 titles)

Novak DJOKOVIC

15) South Africa: 1 champion (1 title)

Johan KRIEK* (South African when he won his first Australian Open in 1981, then he was a US citizen for his second title at the Australian Open in 1982)

25 DIFFERENT COUNTRIES

*Johan KRIEK is the only champion who has been quoted twice in this statistic, for having been victorious under two different citizenships.

Combined Women Champions and Men Champions by Particular Countries

1) USA: 91
2) Australia: 51
3) United Kingdom: 34
4) France: 31
5) Spain: 10
6) Czech Republic: 7
6) Germany: 7
8) Ireland: 6
9) Russia: 5
9) Sweden: 5
11) Argentina: 4
11) Italy: 4
13) Croatia: 3
13) Serbia: 3
13) Switzerland: 3
16) Belgium: 2
16) Brazil: 2
16) Hungary: 2
16) Netherlands: 2
16) Romania: 2
21) Austria: 1
21) Belarus: 1
21) Chile: 1
21) China: 1
21) Ecuador: 1
21) Egypt: 1
21) Mexico: 1
21) New Zealand: 1
21) Norway: 1
21) Slovenia: 1
21) South Africa: 1

31 DIFFERENT COUNTRIES

(4 champions have been quoted twice here, for having won titles under two different citizenships)

Countries with the most titles (women and men, combined)

929 Grand Slam titles have been played, to date:

1) USA: 346
2) Australia: 162
3) United Kingdom: 91
4) France: 89
5) Germany: 37
6) Spain: 30
7) Sweden: 26
8) Switzerland: 24
9) Czech Republic: 21
10) Serbia: 19
11) Russia: 12
12) Belgium: 11
13) Brazil: 10
14) Ireland: 8
15) Argentina: 7
16) New Zealand: 6
17) Italy: 5
18) Croatia: 3
18) Egypt: 3
18) Romania: 3
21) Belarus: 2
21) China: 2
21) Hungary: 2
21) Netherlands: 2
21) Norway: 2
26) Austria: 1
26) Chile: 1
26) Ecuador: 1
26) Mexico: 1
26) Slovenia: 1
26) South Africa: 1

MORE ON CHAMPIONS

All Women Champions over the years

Nelly ADAMSON LANDRY
(Dec. 28, 1916 – Feb. 22, 2010) (Belgium then France) (by marriage)

Daphne AKHURST COZENS
(Apr. 22, 1903 – Jan. 09, 1933) (Australia) (The Australian Open's trophy is named after her)

Juliette ATKINSON
(Apr. 15, 1873 – Jan. 12, 1944) (USA)

Cilly AUSSEM
(Jan. 04, 1909 – Mar. 22, 1963) (Germany)

Tracy AUSTIN
(Dec. 12, 1962) (USA)

Victoria AZARENKA
(Jul. 31, 1989) (Belarus)

Maud BARGER WALLACH
(Jun. 15, 1870 – Apr. 02, 1954) (USA)

Sue BARKER
(Apr. 19, 1956) (UK)

Marion BARTOLI
(Oct. 02, 1984) (France)

Pauline BETZ ADDIE
(Aug. 06, 1919 – May 31, 2011) (USA)

Blanche BINGLEY HILLYARD
(Nov. 03, 1863 – Aug. 06, 1946) (UK)

Molla BJURSTEDT MALLORY
(Mar. 06, 1884 – Nov. 22, 1959) (Norway then USA)

Shirley BLOOMER
(Jun. 13, 1934) (UK)

Dora BOOTHBY
(Aug. 02, 1881 – Feb. 22, 1970) (UK)

Kornelia BOUMAN
(Nov. 23, 1903 – Nov. 17, 1998) (Netherlands)

Esna BOYD ROBERTSON
(Sep. 21, 1899 – 1966) (Australia)

Marguerite BROQUEDIS
(Apr. 17, 1893 – Apr. 23, 1983) (France)

Louise BROUGH CLAPP
(Mar. 11, 1923 – Feb. 03, 2014) (USA)

Maria BUENO
(Oct. 11, 1939) (Brazil)

Dorothy BUNDY CHENEY
(Sep. 01, 1916 – Nov. 23, 2014) (USA) (May Sutton Bundy's daughter)

Mabel CAHILL
(Apr. 02, 1863 – Jan. 01, 1905) (Ireland)

Patricia CANNING TODD
(Jul. 22, 1922 – Sep. 05, 2015) (USA)

Jennifer CAPRIATI
(Mar. 29, 1976) (USA)

Mary CARTER REITANO
(Nov. 29, 1934) (Australia)

Kim CLIJSTERS
(Jun. 08, 1983) (Belgium)

Maureen CONNOLLY
(Sep. 17, 1934 – Jun. 21, 1969) (USA)

Charlotte COOPER STERRY
(Sep. 22, 1870 – Oct 10, 1966) (UK)

Thelma COYNE LONG
(Oct. 14, 1918 – Apr. 13, 2015) (Australia)

Lindsay DAVENPORT
(Jun. 08, 1976) (USA)

Lottie DOD
(Sep. 24, 1871 – Jun. 27, 1960) (UK)

Françoise DURR
(Dec. 25, 1942) (France)

Chris EVERT
(Dec. 21, 1954) (USA)

Shirley FRY IRVIN
(Jun. 30, 1927) (USA)

Althea GIBSON
(Aug. 25, 1927 – Sep. 28, 2003) (USA)

Kate GILLOU FENWICK
(Feb. 19, 1887 – Feb. 16, 1964) (France)

P. GIROD
(France)

Evonne GOOLAGONG-CAWLEY
(Jul. 31, 1951) (Australia)

Steffi GRAF
(Jun. 14, 1969) (Germany) (Married Andre Agassi, following her retirement)

Ellen HANSELL
(Sep. 18, 1869 – May 11, 1937) (USA)

Karen HANTZE SUSMAN
(Dec. 11, 1942) (USA)

Darlene HARD
(Jan. 06, 1936) (USA)

Doris HART
(Jun. 20, 1925 – May 29, 2015) (USA)

Joan HARTIGAN BATHURST
(Jun 06, 1912 – Aug 31, 2000) (Australia)

Ann HAYDON-JONES
(Oct. 07, 1938) (UK)

Helen HELLWIG
(Mar.1874 – Nov. 26, 1960) (USA)

Justine HENIN
(Jun. 01, 1982) (Belgium)

Martina HINGIS
(Sep. 30, 1980) (Switzerland)

Helen HOMANS
(1878 or 1879 – Mar. 29, 1949) (USA)

Emily HOOD WESTACOOT
(May 06, 1910 – Oct. 09, 1980) (Australia)

Hazel HOTCHKISS WIGHTMAN
(Dec. 20, 1886 – Dec. 05, 1974) (USA)

Helen HULL JACOBS
(Aug. 06, 1908 – Jun. 02, 1997) (USA)

Ana IVANOVIC
(Nov. 06, 1987) (Serbia)

Mima JAUSOVEC
(Jul. 20, 1956) (Yugoslavia – Slovenia)

Marion JONES FARQUHAR
(Nov. 02, 1879 – Mar. 14, 1965) (USA)

Barbara JORDAN
(Apr. 02, 1957) (USA)

Mary KENDALL BROWNE
(Jun. 03, 1891 – Aug. 19, 1971) (USA)

Thérèse de KERMEL (Countess) (née Villard)
(Jun. 15, 1874 – 1955) (France)

Billie Jean KING (née Moffitt)
(Nov. 22, 1943) (USA)

Zsuzsa KORMOCZY
(Aug. 25, 1924 – Sep. 16, 2006) (Hungary)

Hilde KRAHWINKEL SPERLING
(Mar. 26, 1908 – Mar. 07, 1981) (Germany then Denmark) (by marriage)

Svetlana KUZNETSOVA
(Jun. 27, 1985) (Russia)

Petra KVITOVA
(Mar. 08, 1990) (Czech Republic)

Dorothea LAMBERT-CHAMBERS (née Douglass)
(Sep. 03, 1878 – Jan. 07, 1960) (UK)

Sylvia LANCE HARPER
(Oct.1895 - deceased) (Australia)

Suzanne LENGLEN
(May 24, 1899 – Jul. 04, 1938) (France)

Na LI
(Feb. 26, 1982) (China)

Anita LIZANA
(Nov. 19, 1915 – Aug. 21, 1994) (Chile)

Iva MAJOLI
(Aug. 12, 1977) (Croatia)

Hana MANDLIKOVA
(Feb. 19, 1962) (Czechoslovakia (Czech Republic) then Australia after her retirement)

Alice MARBLE
(Sep. 28, 1913 – Dec. 13, 1990) (USA)

Conchita MARTINEZ
(Apr. 16, 1972) (Spain)

Adine MASSON
(France)

Simonne MATHIEU
(Jan. 31, 1908 – Jan. 07, 1980) (France)

Jeanne MATTHEY
(France)

Amélie MAURESMO
(Jul. 05, 1979) (France)

Myrtle McATEER
(Jun. 12, 1878 – Oct. 26, 1952) (USA)

Coral McINNES BUTTSWORTH
(1900 – Dec. 20, 1985) (Australia)

Kathleen McKANE GODFREE
(May 07, 1896 – Jun. 19, 1992) (UK)

Kerry MELVILLE REID
(Aug. 07, 1947) (Australia)

Margaret MOLESWORTH
(1894 – Jul. 09, 1985) (Australia)

Elisabeth MOORE
(Mar. 05, 1876 – Jan. 22, 1959) (USA)

Angela MORTIMER
(Apr. 21, 1932) (UK)

Anastasia MYSKINA
(Jul. 08, 1981) (Russia)

Martina NAVRATILOVA
(Oct. 18, 1956) (Czechoslovakia (Czech Republic) then USA)

Jana NOVOTNA
(Oct. 02, 1968) (Czechoslovakia – Czech Republic)

Betty NUTHALL
(May 23, 1911 – Nov. 08, 1983) (UK)

Chris O'NEIL
(Mar. 19, 1956) (Australia)

Margaret OSBORNE duPONT
(Mar. 04, 1918 – Oct. 24, 2012) (USA)

Sarah PALFREY COOKE
(Sep. 18, 1912 – Feb. 27, 1996) (USA) (Her brother John married Theodore Roosevelt's granddaughter)

Flavia PENNETTA
(Feb. 25, 1982) (Italy)

Beryl PENROSE
(Dec. 22, 1930) (Australia)

Mary PIERCE
(Jan. 15, 1975) (France, Canada, USA)

Hélène PREVOST
(France)

Lena RICE
(Jun. 21, 1866 – Jun. 21, 1907) (Ireland)

Nancy RICHEY
(Aug. 23, 1942) (USA)

Muriel ROBB
(May 13, 1878 – Feb. 12, 1907) (UK)

Ellen ROOSEVELT
(Aug. 20, 1868 – Sep. 26, 1954) (USA) (Franklin D.Roosevelt's cousin)

Dorothy ROUND LITTLE
(Jul. 13, 1908 – Nov. 12, 1982) (UK)

Virginia RUZICI
(Jan. 31, 1955) (Romania)

Gabriela SABATINI
(May 16, 1970) (Argentina)

Arantxa SANCHEZ VICARIO
(Dec. 18, 1971) (Spain)

Francesca SCHIAVONE
(Jun. 23, 1980) (Italy)

Margaret SCRIVEN
(Aug. 17, 1912 – Jan. 25, 2001) (UK)

Evelyn SEARS
(Mar. 09, 1875 – Nov. 10, 1966) (USA)

Monica SELES
(Dec. 02, 1973) (Yugoslavia (Serbia) then USA)

Maria SHARAPOVA
(Apr. 19, 1987) (Russia)

Margaret SMITH COURT
(Jul. 16, 1942) (Australia)

Samantha STOSUR
(Mar. 30, 1984) (Australia)

May SUTTON BUNDY
(Sep. 25, 1886 – Oct. 04, 1975) (USA) (Dorothy Bundy Cheney's mother)

Aline TERRY
(USA)

Ethel THOMSON LARCOMBE
(Jun. 08, 1879 – Aug. 11, 1965) (UK)

Bertha TOWNSEND
(Mar. 07, 1869 – May 12, 1909) (USA)

Christine TRUMAN
(Jan. 16, 1941) (UK)

Lesley TURNER BOWREY
(Aug. 16, 1942) (Australia) (Wife of champion Bill Bowrey)

Julie VLASTO
(Aug. 08, 1903 – Mar. 02, 1985) (France)

Virginia WADE
(Jul. 10, 1945) (UK)

Maud WATSON
(Oct. 09, 1864 – Jun. 05, 1946) (UK)

Serena WILLIAMS
(Sep. 26, 1981) (USA)

Venus WILLIAMS
(Jun. 17, 1980) (USA)

Helen WILLS MOODY
(Oct. 06, 1905 – Jan. 01, 1998) (USA)

Nancye WYNNE BOLTON
(Dec. 02, 1916 – Nov. 09, 2001) (Australia)

The oldest Grand Slam's champion alive is Shirley Fry Irvin, born June 30, 1927, 88 years old.

The youngest Grand Slam's champion still playing is Petra Kvitova, born March 8, 1990, 25 years old.

They are 62 years and 8 months apart.

All Men Champions over the years

Andre AGASSI
(Apr. 29, 1970) (USA) (Married Steffi Graf following his retirement)

Fred ALEXANDER
(Aug. 14, 1880 – Mar. 03, 1969) (USA)

Wilmer ALLISON
(Dec. 08, 1904 – Apr. 20, 1977) (USA)

James ANDERSON
(Sep. 17, 1894 – Dec. 23, 1973) (Australia)

Mal ANDERSON
(Mar. 03, 1935) (Australia)

Jozsef ASBOTH
(Sep. 18, 1917 – Sep. 22, 1986) (Hungary)

Arthur ASHE
(Jul. 10, 1943 – Feb. 06, 1993) (USA)

Paul AYME
(Jul. 29, 1869 – Jul. 25, 1962) (France)

Wilfred BADDELEY
(Jan. 11, 1872 – Jan. 24, 1929) (UK)

Boris BECKER
(Nov. 22, 1967) (Germany)

Marcel BERNARD
(May 18, 1914 – Apr. 29, 1994) (France)

François BLANCHY
(Dec. 12, 1886 – Oct. 02, 1960) (France)

Björn BORG
(Jun. 06, 1956) (Sweden)

Jean BOROTRA
(Aug. 13, 1898 – Jul. 17, 1994) (France)

Bill BOWREY
(Dec. 25, 1943) (Australia) (Husband of champion Lesley Turner)

H. BRIGGS
(UK)

John BROMWICH
(Nov. 14, 1918 – Oct. 21, 1999) (Australia)

Norman BROOKES (Sir)
(Nov. 14, 1877 – Sep. 28, 1968) (Australia) (The Australian Open Trophy is named after him)

Sergi BRUGUERA
(Jan. 16, 1971) (Spain)

Donald BUDGE
(Jun. 13, 1915 – Jan. 26, 2000) (USA)

Oliver CAMPBELL
(Feb. 25, 1871 – Jul. 11, 1953) (USA)

Pat CASH
(May 27, 1965) (Australia)

Michael CHANG
(Feb. 22, 1972) (USA)

Marin CILIC
(Sep. 28, 1988) (Croatia)

William CLOTHIER
(Sep. 27, 1881 – Sep. 04, 1962) (USA)

Henri COCHET
(Dec. 14, 1901 – Apr. 01, 1987) (France)

Jimmy CONNORS
(Sep. 02, 1952) (USA)

Ashley COOPER
(Sep. 15, 1936) (Australia)

Albert COSTA
(Jun. 25, 1975) (Spain)

Jim COURIER
(Aug. 17, 1970) (USA)

Jack CRAWFORD
(Mar. 22, 1908 – Sep. 10, 1991) (Australia)

Sven DAVIDSON
(Jul. 13, 1928 – May 28, 2008) (Sweden)

Max DECUGIS
(Sep. 24, 1882 – Sep. 06, 1978) (France)

Juan Martin DEL POTRO
(Sep. 23, 1988) (Argentina)

Novak DJOKOVIC
(May 22, 1987) (Serbia)

John DOEG
(Dec. 07, 1908 – Apr. 27, 1978) (USA)

Laurie DOHERTY
(Oct. 08, 1875 – Aug. 21, 1919) (UK)

Reggie DOHERTY
(Oct. 14, 1872 – Dec. 29, 1910) (UK)

Jaroslav DROBNY
(Oct. 12, 1921 – Sep. 13, 2001) (Czechoslovakia then "Protectorate of Bohemia and Moravia" (during WWII), then Egypt, then UK)

Stefan EDBERG
(Jan. 19, 1966) (Sweden)

Mark EDMONDSON

(Jun. 24, 1954) (Australia)

Roy EMERSON
(Nov. 03, 1936) (Australia)

Bob FALKENBURG
(Jan. 29, 1926) (USA)

Roger FEDERER
(Aug. 08, 1981) (Switzerland)

Juan Carlos FERRERO
(Feb. 12, 1980) (Spain)

Neale FRASER
(Oct. 03, 1933) (Australia)

Gaston GAUDIO
(Dec. 09, 1978) (Argentina)

Rhys GEMMELL
(1896 – deceased) (Australia)

Maurice GERMOT
(Nov. 15, 1882 – Aug. 06, 1958) (France)

Vitas GERULAITIS
(Jul. 26, 1954 – Sep. 17, 1994) (USA)

Andres GIMENO
(Aug. 03, 1937) (Spain)

André GOBERT
(Sep. 14, 1890 – Dec. 06, 1951) (France)

Andres GOMEZ
(Feb. 27, 1960) (Ecuador)

Pancho GONZALEZ
(May 09, 1928 – Jul. 03, 1995) (USA)

Arthur GORE

(Jan. 02, 1868 – Dec. 01, 1928) (UK)

Spencer GORE
(Mar. 10, 1850 – Apr. 19, 1906) (UK)

Colin GREGORY (Doctor)
(Jul. 28, 1903 – Jan. 10, 1959) (UK)

Frank HADOW
(Jan. 24, 1855 – Jun. 29, 1946) (UK)

Willoughby HAMILTON
(Dec. 09, 1864 – Sep. 27, 1943) (Ireland)

John HARTLEY
(Jan. 09, 1849 – Aug. 21, 1935) (UK)

John HAWKES
(Jun. 07, 1899 – Mar. 31, 1990) (Australia)

Rodney HEATH
(Jun. 15, 1884 – Oct. 06, 1936) (Australia)

Henner HENKEL
(Oct. 09, 1915 – Jan. 13, 1943) (Germany) (Died on the battlefield, Stalingrad)

Lleyton HEWITT
(Feb. 24, 1981) (Australia)

Lewis HOAD
(Nov. 23, 1934 – Jul. 03, 1994) (Australia)

Fred HOVEY
(Oct. 07, 1868 – Oct. 18, 1945) (USA)

Joseph HUNT
(Feb. 17, 1919 – Feb. 02, 1945) (USA)

Goran IVANISEVIC
(Sep. 13, 1971) (Croatia)

Thomas JOHANSSON

(Mar. 24, 1975) (Sweden)

Bill JOHNSTON
(Nov. 02, 1894 – May 01, 1946) (USA)

Yevgeny KAFELNIKOV
(Feb. 18, 1974) (Russia)

Algernon KINGSCOTE
(Dec. 03, 1888 – Dec. 21, 1964) (UK)

Jan KODES
(Mar. 01, 1946) (Czechoslovakia – Czech Republic)

Petr KORDA
(Jan. 23, 1968) (Czech Republic)

Richard KRAJICEK
(Dec. 06, 1971) (Netherlands)

Jack KRAMER
(Aug. 01, 1921 – Sep. 12, 2009) (USA)

Johan KRIEK
(Apr. 05, 1958) (South Africa then USA)

Gustavo KUERTEN
(Sep. 10, 1976) (Brazil)

René LACOSTE
(Jul. 02, 1904 – Oct. 12, 1996) (Francc)

William LARNED
(Dec. 30, 1872 – Dec. 16, 1926) (USA)

Arthur LARSEN
(Apr. 17, 1925 – Dec. 07, 2012) (USA)

Rod LAVER
(Aug. 09, 1938) (Australia)

Herbert LAWFORD

(May 15, 1851 – Apr. 20, 1925) (UK)

Ivan LENDL
(Mar. 07, 1960) (Czechoslovakia (Czech Republic) then USA)

Gordon LOWE (Sir) (2nd Baronet)
(Jun. 21, 1884 – May 17, 1972) (UK)

Harold MAHONY
(Feb. 13, 1867 – Jun. 27, 1905) (Ireland)

John McENROE
(Feb. 16, 1959) (USA)

Vivian McGRATH
(Feb. 17, 1916 – Apr. 09, 1978) (Australia)

Ken McGREGOR
(Jun. 02, 1929 – Dec. 01, 2007) (Australia)

Chuck McKINLEY
(Jan. 05, 1941 – Aug. 10, 1986) (USA)

Maurice McLOUGHLIN
(Jan. 07, 1890 – Dec. 10, 1957) (USA)

William McNEILL
(Apr. 30, 1918 – Nov. 28, 1996) (USA)

Edgar MOON
(Dec. 03, 1904 – May 26, 1976) (Australia)

Carlos MOYA
(Aug. 27, 1976) (Spain)

Andy MURRAY
(May 15, 1987) (UK)

Robert Lindley MURRAY
(Nov. 03, 1892 – Jan. 17, 1970) (USA)

Thomas MUSTER

(Oct. 02, 1967) (Austria)

Rafael NADAL
(Jun. 03, 1986) (Spain)

Ilie NASTASE
(Jul. 19, 1946) (Romania)

John NEWCOMBE
(May 23, 1944) (Australia)

Yannick NOAH
(May 18, 1960) (France)

Arthur O'HARA WOOD
(1890 – Oct. 06, 1918) (Australia) (Died on the battlefield, WWI in France) (Pat O'Hara Wood's brother)

Pat O'HARA WOOD
(Apr. 30, 1891 – Dec. 03, 1961) (Australia) (Arthur O'Hara Wood's brother)

Alex OLMEDO
(Mar. 24, 1936) (Peru then USA)

Manuel ORANTES
(Feb. 05, 1949) (Spain)

Rafael OSUNA
(Sep. 15, 1938 – Jun. 04, 1969) (Mexico) (Died in flight Mexicana 704 crash, 79 victims)

Dinny PAILS
(Mar. 04, 1921   Nov. 22, 1986) (Australia)

Adriano PANATTA
(Jul. 09, 1950) (Italy)

James PARKE
(Jul. 26, 1881 – Feb. 27, 1946) (Ireland)

Ernie PARKER
(Nov. 05, 1883 – May 02, 1918) (Australia) (Died on the battlefield, WWI in France)

Frank PARKER

(Jan. 31, 1916 – Jul. 24, 1997) (USA)

Gerald PATTERSON
(Dec. 17, 1895 – Jun. 13, 1967) (Australia)

Budge PATTY
(Feb. 11, 1924) (USA)

Fred PERRY
(May 18, 1909 – Feb. 02, 1995) (UK)

Yvon PETRA
(Mar. 08, 1916 – Sep. 12, 1984) (France)

Nicola PIETRANGELI
(Sep. 11, 1933) (Italy)

Joshua PIM (Doctor)
(May 20, 1869 – Apr. 15, 1942) (Ireland)

Adrian QUIST
(Jan. 23, 1913 – Nov. 17, 1991) (Australia)

Patrick RAFTER
(Dec. 28, 1972) (Australia)

Ernest RENSHAW
(Jan. 03, 1861 – Sep. 02, 1899) (UK) (Born 15min before his twin brother William)

William RENSHAW
(Jan. 03, 1861 – Aug. 12, 1904) (UK) (Born 15min after his twin brother Ernest)

Laurent RIBOULET
(Apr. 18, 1871 – Sep. 04, 1960) (France)

Horace RICE
(Sep. 05, 1873 – 1950) (Australia)

Bobby RIGGS
(Feb. 25, 1918 – Oct. 25, 1995) (USA)

Tony ROCHE

(May 17, 1945) (Australia)

Andy RODDICK
(Aug. 30, 1982) (USA)

Mervyn ROSE
(Jan. 23, 1930) (Australia)

Ken ROSEWALL
(Nov. 02, 1934) (Australia)

Marat SAFIN
(Jan. 27, 1980) (Russia)

Jean SAMAZEUILH
(Jan. 17, 1891 – Apr. 13, 1965) (France)

Pete SAMPRAS
(Aug. 12, 1971) (USA)

Manuel SANTANA
(May 10, 1938) (Spain)

Dick SAVITT
(Mar. 04, 1927) (USA)

Jean SCHOPFER
(May 28, 1868 – Jan. 09, 1931) (France)

Ted SCHROEDER
(Jul. 20, 1921 – May 26, 2006) (USA)

Richard SEARS
(Oct. 16, 1861 – Apr. 08, 1943) (USA)

Frank SEDGMAN
(Oct. 29, 1927) (Australia)

Vic SEIXAS
(Aug. 30, 1923) (USA)

Henry SLOCUM

(May 28, 1862 – Jan. 22, 1949) (USA)

Stan SMITH
(Dec. 14, 1946) (USA)

Michael STICH
(Oct. 18, 1968) (Germany)

Fred STOLLE
(Oct. 08, 1938) (Australia)

Roscoe TANNER
(Oct. 15, 1951) (USA)

Brian TEACHER
(Dec. 23, 1954) (USA)

William TILDEN
(Feb. 10, 1893 – Jun. 05, 1953) (USA)

Tony TRABERT
(Aug. 16, 1930) (USA)

André VACHEROT
(Aug. 27, 1860 – Mar. 22, 1950) (France) (Michel Vacherot's brother)

Michel VACHEROT
(Nov. 12, 1864 – Mar. 22, 1959) (France) (André Vacherot's brother)

Guillermo VILAS
(Aug. 17, 1952) (Argentina)

Ellsworth VINES
(Sep. 28, 1911 – Mar. 17, 1994) (USA)

Gottfried von CRAMM (Baron)
(Jul. 07, 1909 – Nov. 08, 1976) (Germany)

Holcombe WARD
(Nov. 23, 1878 – Jan. 23, 1967) (USA)

Stanislas WAWRINKA

(Mar. 28, 1985) (Switzerland)

Malcolm WHITMAN
(Mar. 15, 1877 – Dec. 28, 1932) (USA)

Mats WILANDER
(Aug. 22, 1964) (Sweden)

Tony WILDING
(Oct. 31, 1883 – May 09, 1915) (New-Zealand) (Died on the battlefield, WWI in France)

Richard Norris WILLIAMS
(Jan. 29, 1891 – Jun. 02, 1968) (USA) (Survivor of RMS Titanic disaster on April 15, 1912)

Sidney WOOD
(Nov. 01, 1911 – Jan. 10, 2009) (USA)

Robert WRENN
(Sep. 20, 1873 – Nov. 21, 1925) (USA)

Beals WRIGHT
(Dec. 19, 1879 – Aug. 23, 1961) (USA)

The oldest Grand Slam's champion alive is Vic Seixas, born August 30, 1923, 92 years old.

The youngest Grand Slam's champion still playing is Marin Cilic, born September 28, 1988, 27 years old.

They are 65 years apart.

TWO CHAMPION SURVIVORS OF THE TITANIC

Tennis fans may not be aware of this, but within the elite of tennis, two champions were survivors of the dreadful Titanic tragedy, on the 15th of April 1912.

Richard Norris Williams, USA (Jan. 29, 1891 – Jun. 02, 1968)

1913 US Championships, final:
Maurice McLoughlin def. **Richard Williams** 6-4, 5-7, 6-3, 6-1
1914 US Championships, final:
Richard Williams def. Maurice McLoughlin 6-3, 8-6, 10-8
1916 US Championships, final:
Richard Williams def. Bill Johnston 4-6, 6-4, 0-6, 6-2, 6-4

This may well be the most astonishing event of tennis history:

In September 1912, Richard Williams won the mixed doubles, with his partner Mary K. Browne at the US Championships (later known as the US Open).
They won the final against William Clothier and Eleonora Sears 6-4, 2-6, 11-9.
Why is this win so exceptional?
Because, **FIVE MONTHS earlier**, on April 15, 1912, the same Richard Williams, aged 21, was one of the 711 survivors of the Titanic tragedy.

Richard and his father Charles Duane Williams (who died that night), were first class passengers on the ship.
After the Titanic sank, Richard Norris Williams was able to reach a lifeboat, and was rescued by the RMS Carpathia in the early morning. The Doctor on board was considering amputating Richard Williams' two legs because of very poor blood circulation. This was caused by the freezing water in his lifeboat; his legs were immersed until the rescue.
Williams, who was very serious in pursuing his tennis career, insisted his legs were left intact and instead chose to walk, day and night on the ship, despite not having any feeling in his legs.

Williams' tenacity saved his legs miraculously and only five months later, safe from this terrible ordeal, he became the winner of the US Championships' mixed doubles with Mary K. Browne!

The year after, in 1913, Williams won the Davis Cup for the USA, with the support of his friend Karl Behr, who was also a survivor of the Titanic!

Richard Norris Williams' two biggest wins in tennis were his two singles titles at the US Championships, during WWI, in 1914 and 1916. The US Championships were the only one of the four major tournaments played during the two World Wars.

Richard Norris Williams died from emphysema on June 2nd, 1968, at the age of 77 years old, in Bryn Mawr, Pennsylvania.

Karl Behr, USA (May 30, 1885 – Oct 15, 1949)

Karl Behr never won nor was he a finalist in the singles category in a Grand Slam tournament, but was a finalist in men's doubles at Wimbledon in 1907.

Behr, along with his friend Williams, was also one of the 711 survivors of the Titanic tragedy, in April 1912, at the age of 26.

Helen Newsom was Karl Behr's girlfriend at the time. Helen's mother was not happy with the relationship and organised a trip to Europe for her daughter, with the intent to separate the couple for a while. Their trip back to the USA was onboard the Titanic.

Karl Behr, who was in love with Newsom, bought his ticket and was on board as well.

After the collision with the iceberg, Behr and Newsom met on the deck and ended up in the same lifeboat. Karl Behr proposed to Helen Newsom in the lifeboat, and they subsequently had four children.

QUIZ: the answers

Answers to questions from the book's introduction:

- In which final was the first grand slam tie-break played?
US Open Men's final, 1970. Ken Rosewall def. Tony Roche 2-6, 6-4, 7-6$^{5\text{-}2}$, 6-3. It is worth noting that, at the time, tie-breaks were played to the best of 5 points (instead of 7). Ken Rosewall won this tie-break by 5 points to 2.

- What is the name of the winner of two grand slam singles men titles, who also survived the Titanic tragedy?
Richard Norris Williams.

- How many different champions have won at least one of each grand slam tournament?
7 men and 10 women.

- Who was the only champion from New-Zealand to date? (this player died on the battlefields of France during WWI)?
Tony Wilding.

- Who has played at Wimbledon under FOUR different citizenships during his career?
Jaroslav Drobny.

- Who has won his grand slam titles under different citizenships? (Be careful… Don't answer too quickly, this is a difficult question!)
Johan Kriek.

- What is the name of the woman champion who is the mother of another woman champion?
May Sutton Bundy and Dorothy Bundy Cheney.

- Who are the woman and man, winners of singles grand slam titles, who became married during their careers? They kept playing singles tournaments for years and also played together in mixed doubles. (Be careful! This is another trick question!).
Bill Bowrey and Lesley Turner Bowrey.

CONCLUSION

I hope you've enjoyed discovering the information and statistics listed in this book (some of which are hardly known).

I've decided to write this book because I am (as you would have gathered) passionate about tennis history.

I also wanted to properly pay tribute to ALL champions of tennis history.

I have noticed younger generations of fans are showing little interest in the sport's events going back 5, 10 or 20 years before they started following tennis, let alone the early stages of the sport...

One can easily be under the impression that current champions are the only ones and the most important in tennis history.

Going back in tennis history, it is tempting to compare the performances of players from yesteryear against the performances of contemporary players, who by comparison appear a lot faster and more powerful.

It becomes easy to insinuate wins from back then were "easy".

One has to place every single game back in context. Every player had similar rackets, the same outfits and the same struggles on the way to winning.

It then becomes easier to see how ALL PLAYERS have contributed to making tennis a very popular game.

THANK YOU to all champions for bringing passion into the game. Thank you for making this passion grow within the hearts of fans around the world.

With my sincere gratitude to Jimmy Connors:
My passion for tennis started because of him.
In May 1979, Jimmy Connors returned to Roland-Garros.
It was the first time ever I was watching a tennis game.
His powerful game, his talent and his drive to win will remain vivid in tennis history.
His matches were captivating... thrilling...
Spectators felt as if they were on court with Jimmy.
Thanks to him, I've enjoyed many years of passion for the sport.
Never beaten until the very last ball, Jimmy built a bridge between the court and the spectators' stands, all along his wonderful career.

Beginning in 1970 and officially retiring in 1996 from senior tournaments, Jimmy Connors is the most rewarded player with 109 titles won between 1972 and 1989, including 8 Grand Slam titles.

1991 will remain his most incredible year, with dramatic turnarounds during lengthy, breathtaking matches.

I still envy the fans who saw these matches, live, in 1991, from the US Open stands.

I remember these "impossible " wins against Patrick McEnroe and Aaron Krickstein, then against Paul Haarhuis... with... "THAT POINT"... which electrified the Centre Court.

"THAT POINT", is a summary of Jimmy Connors' game style over three decades.

Thank you Mr Connors, for beginning my fascination with your sport.

Manufactured by Amazon.ca
Acheson, AB